UN-HINGED
A Fantastic Psychedelic
Coloring Book

Featuring All Original
Graphic Designs by
MIKE HINGE

Compiled and with an Introduction by
Jane Frank

ISBN -13: 978-1542654494

ABOUT MIKE HINGE

Welcome to the wonderfully psychedelic, futuristic and surreal world of Mike Hinge, an American artist born in a small town in Auckland, New Zealand. After he moved to Los Angeles, California in 1959, he attended the Art Center of the College of Design . . . and then quickly began applying his skills and imagination to advertising and publishing projects. Mike was a major fan of science fiction in the 1950s, so it was no surprise that he chose to focus on high tech, space and robots.

Mike's distinctive, original graphic style is unforgettable – and the following pages will give you hours of coloring fun! His line drawings and sharply imagined black-and white compositions of beautiful space women, robots on roller skates, and running astronauts are perfect for all fans of the fantastical and techie psychedelic!

For your coloring pleasure, each page has a blank reverse side so you don't have to worry about colors bleeding through, and for easy framing of your coloring projects. As for the rest: just follow Mike's way - be experimental and creative!

Mike Hinge died in 2003, but the illustrations and drawings he created, many of them published in science fiction and fantasy magazines or book covers in the 1960s and 1970s, live on through this book. So let your mind expand, and explore the marvels of Mike Hinge's artistry! Happy coloring!

Jane Frank

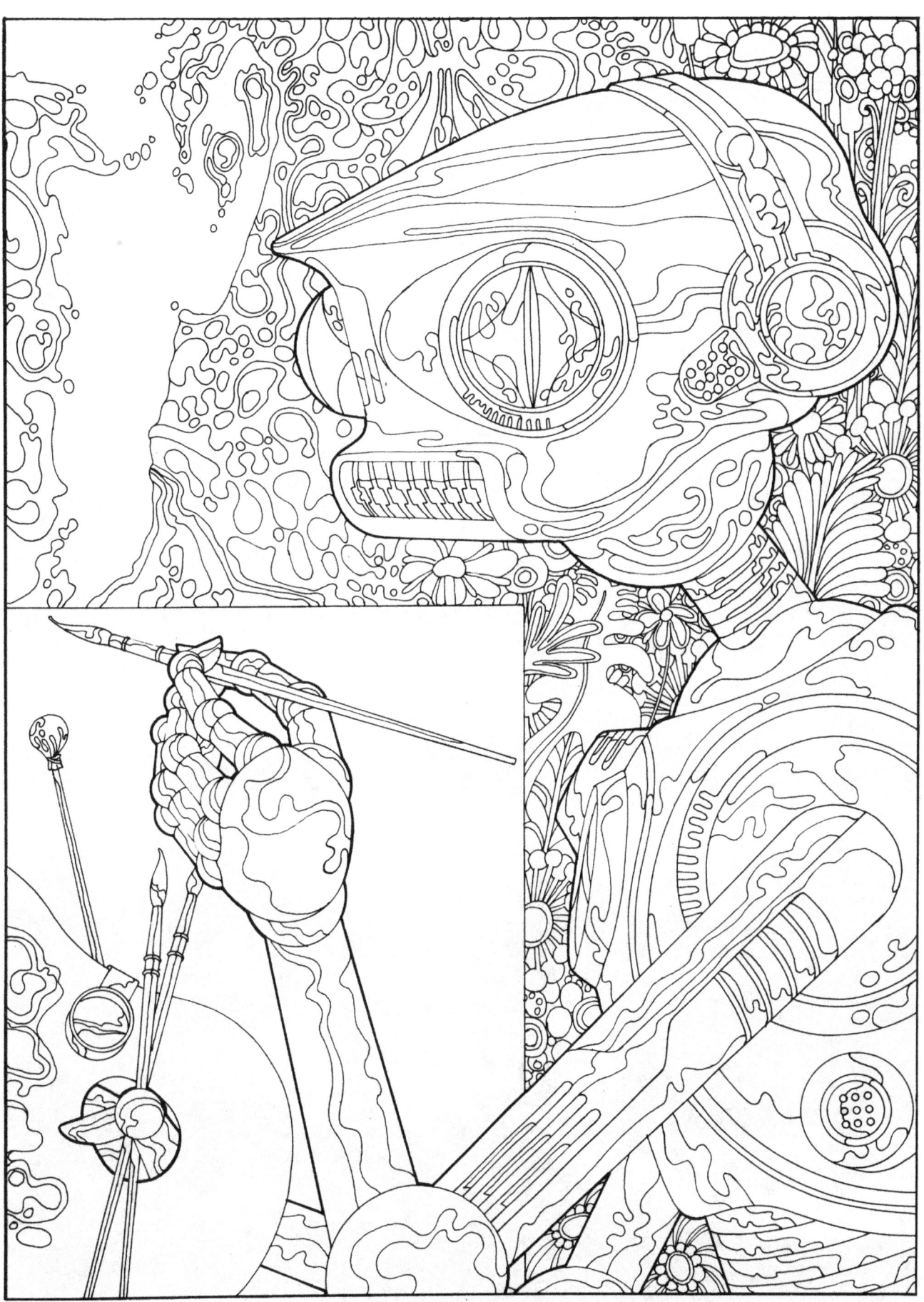

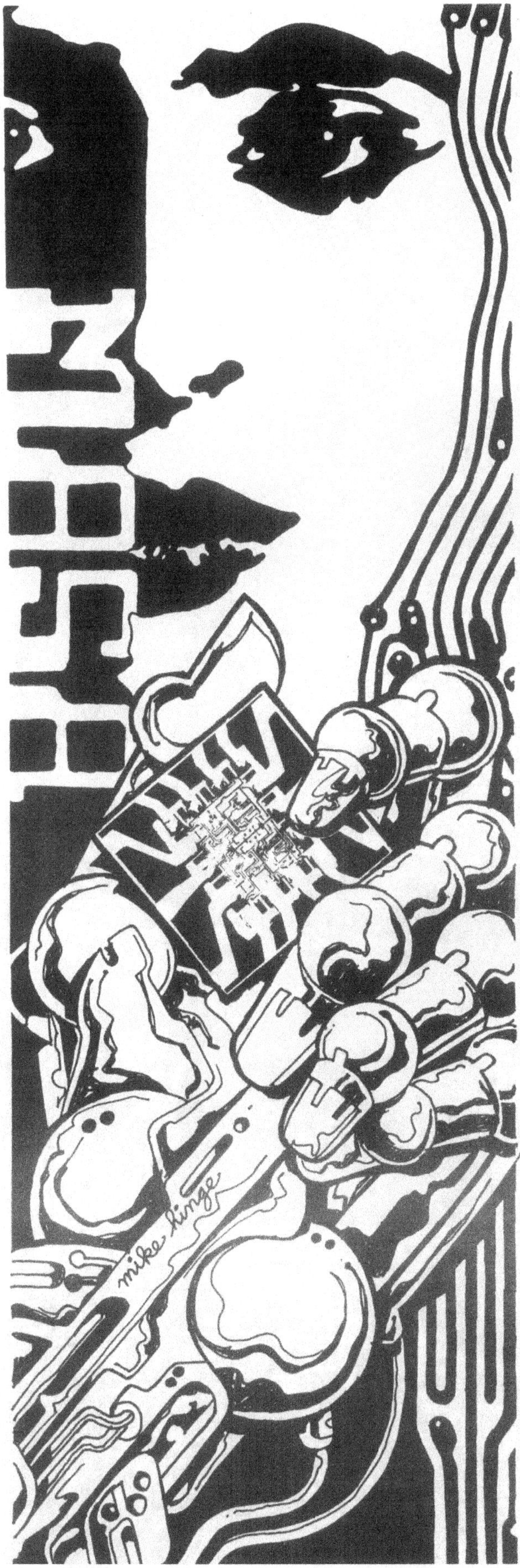

mike hinge

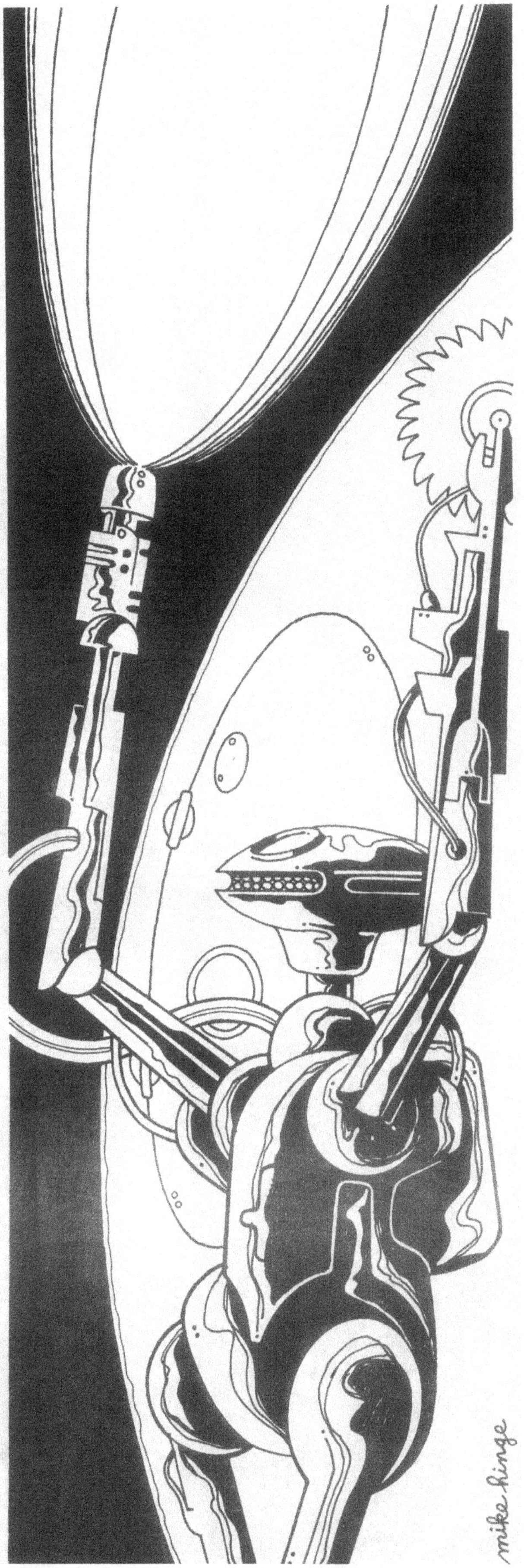

mike hinge

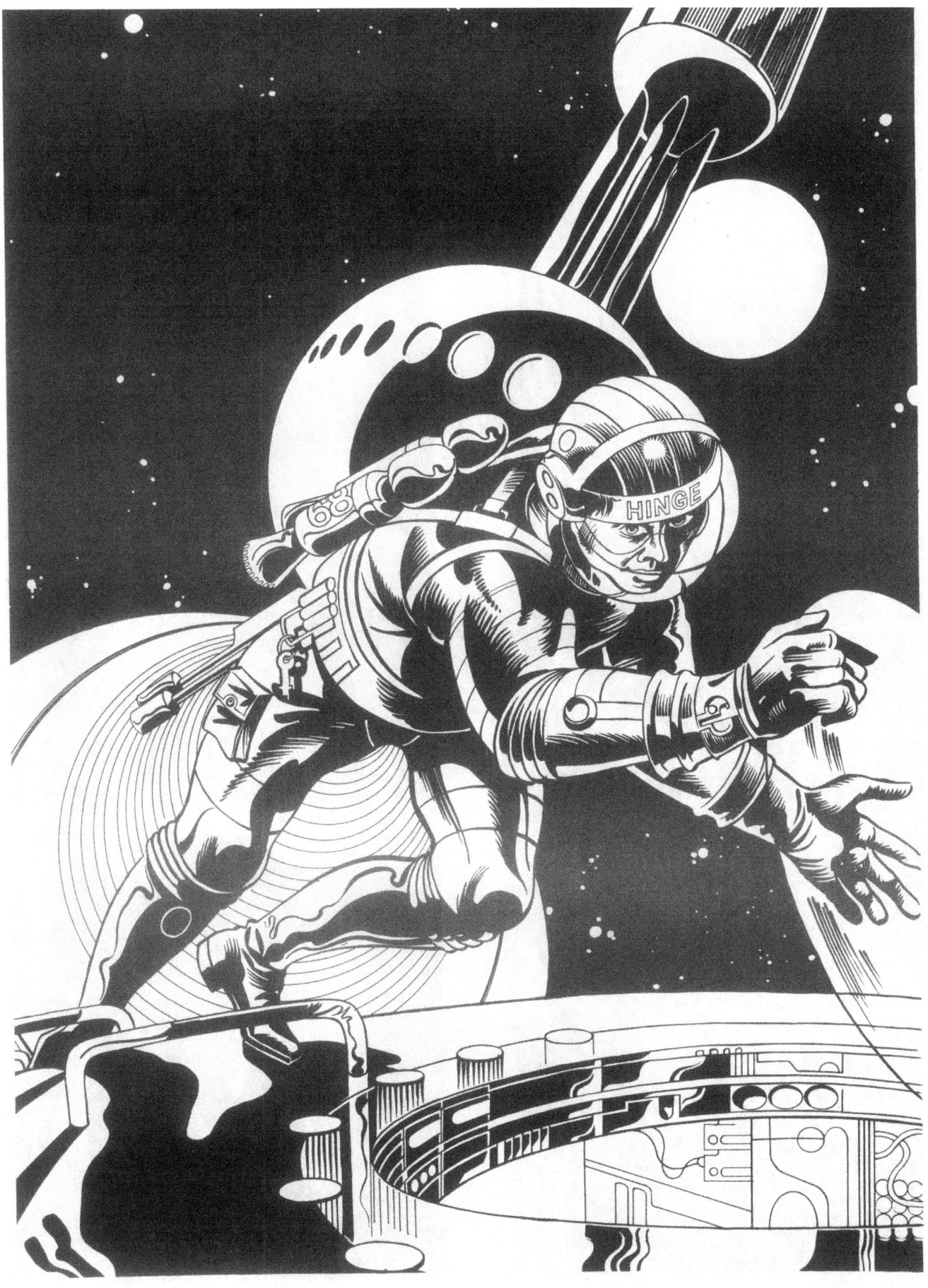

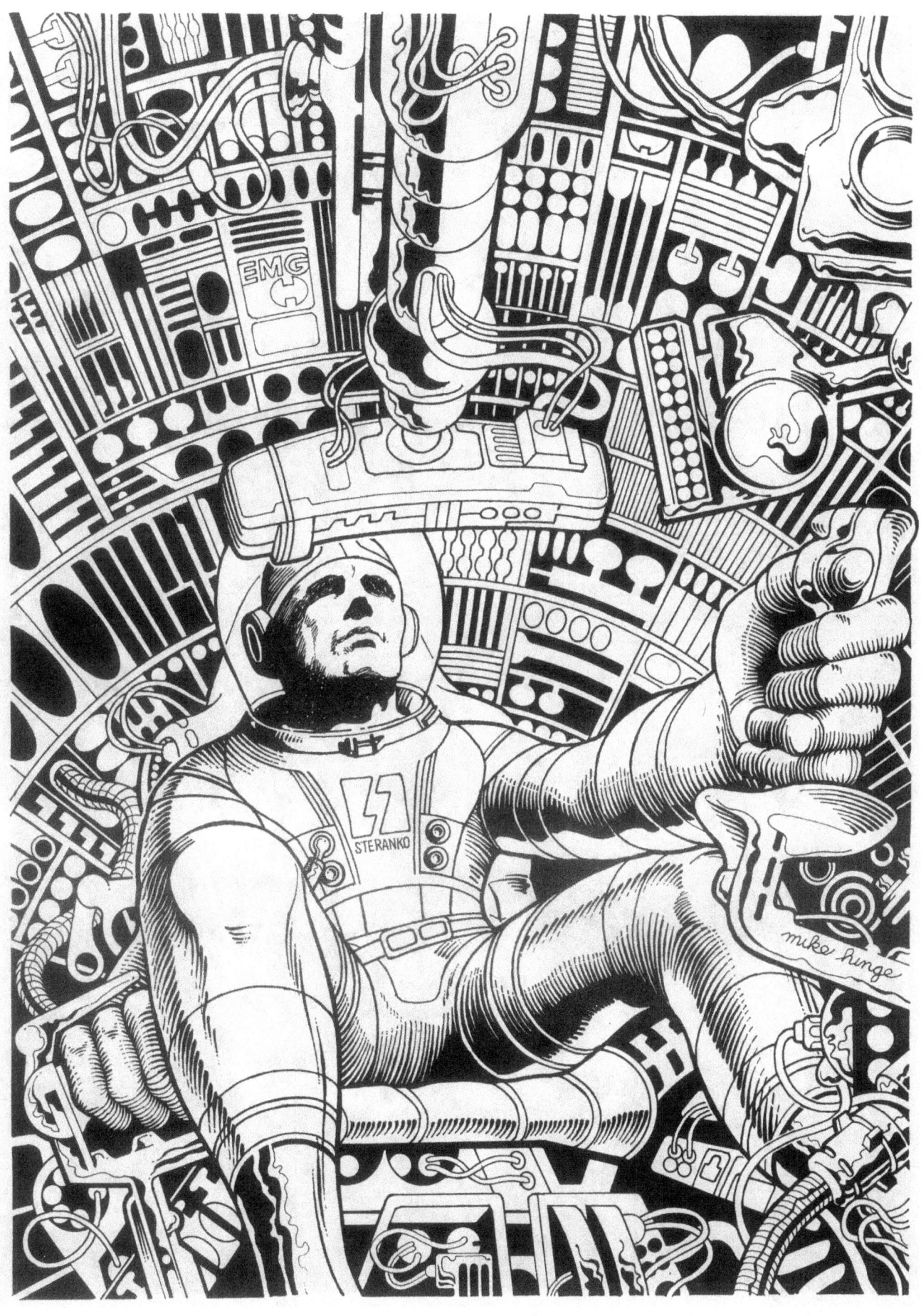

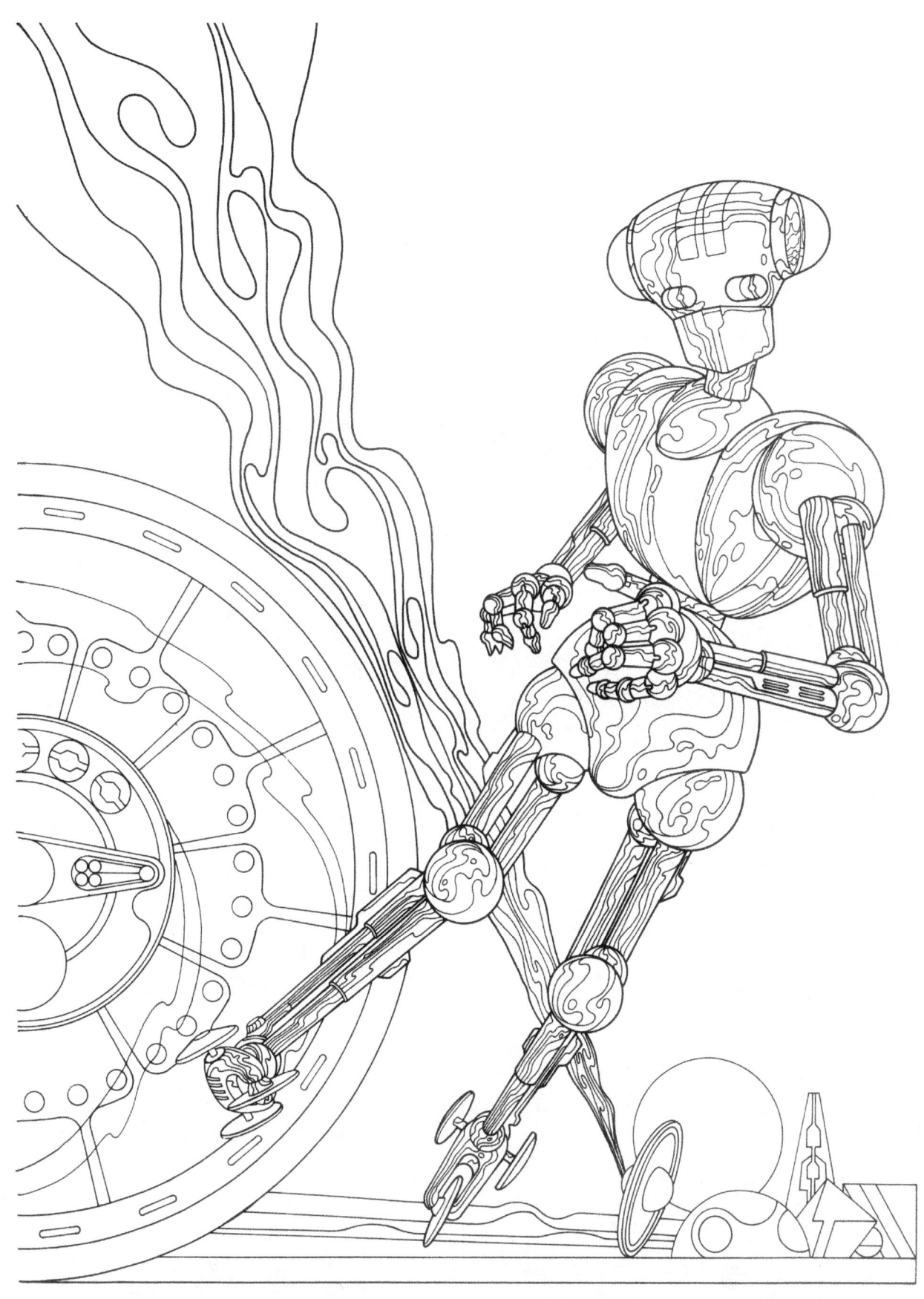

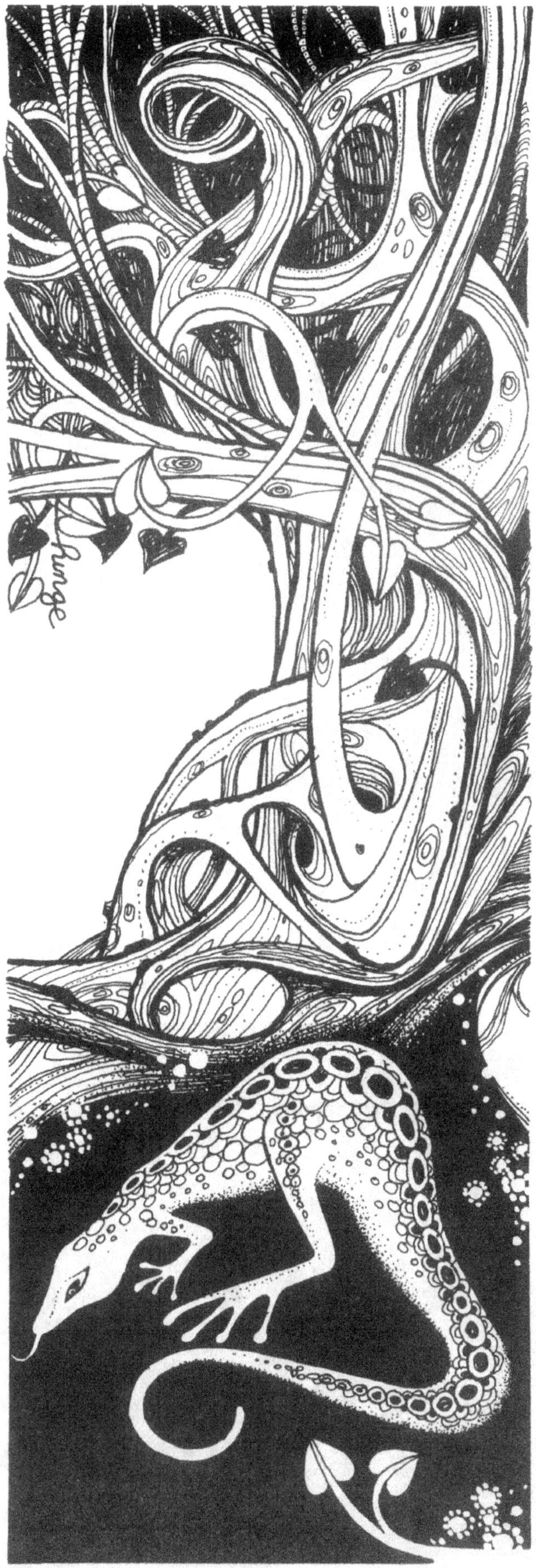

mike hinge

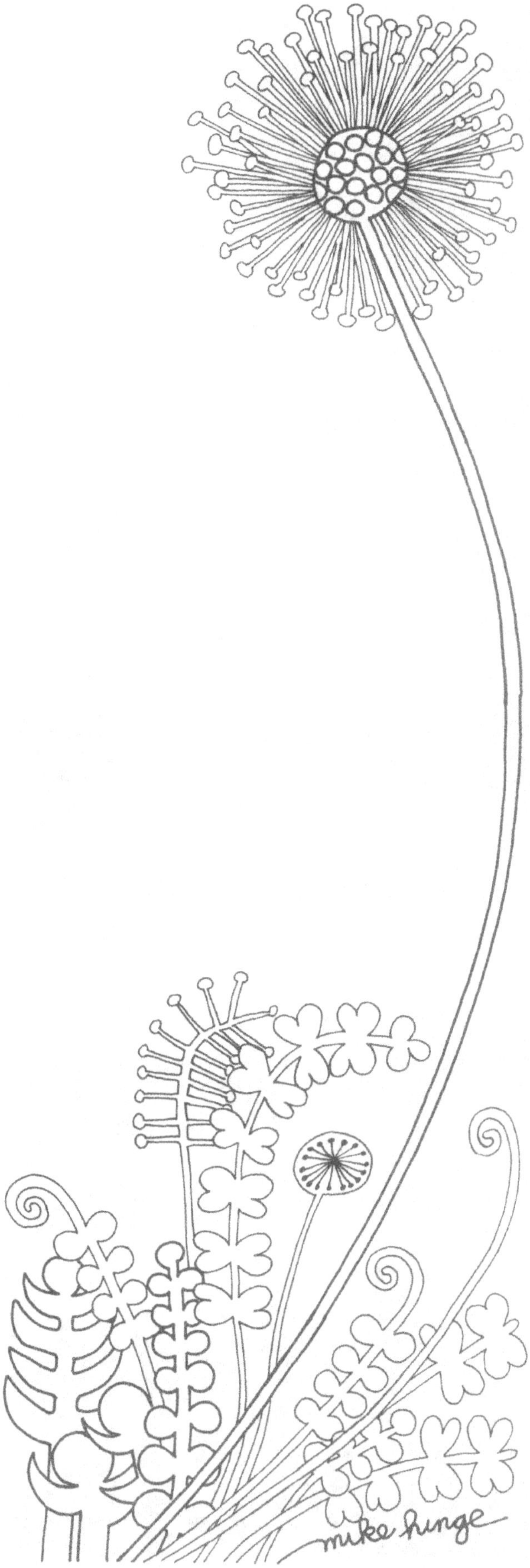

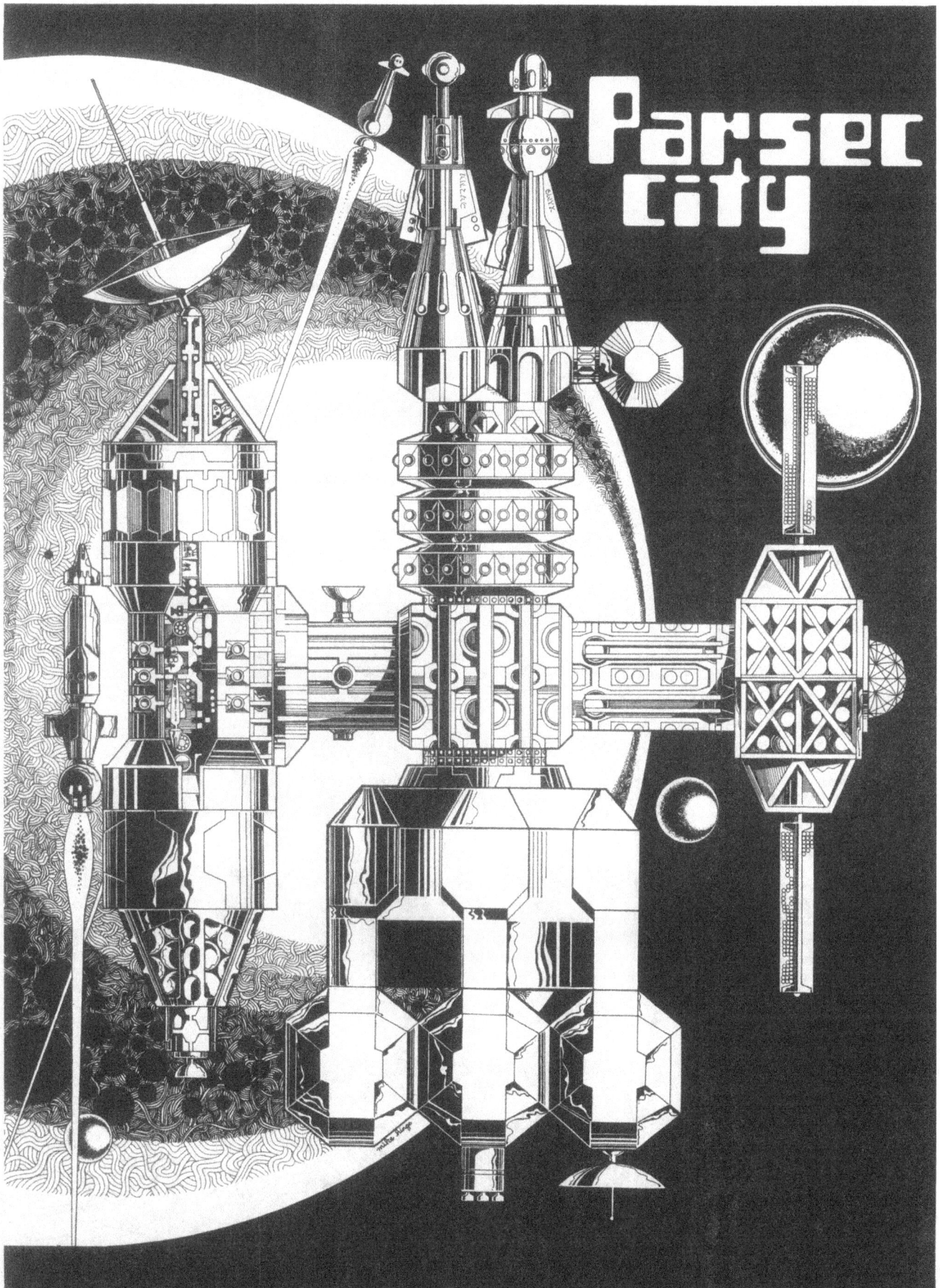

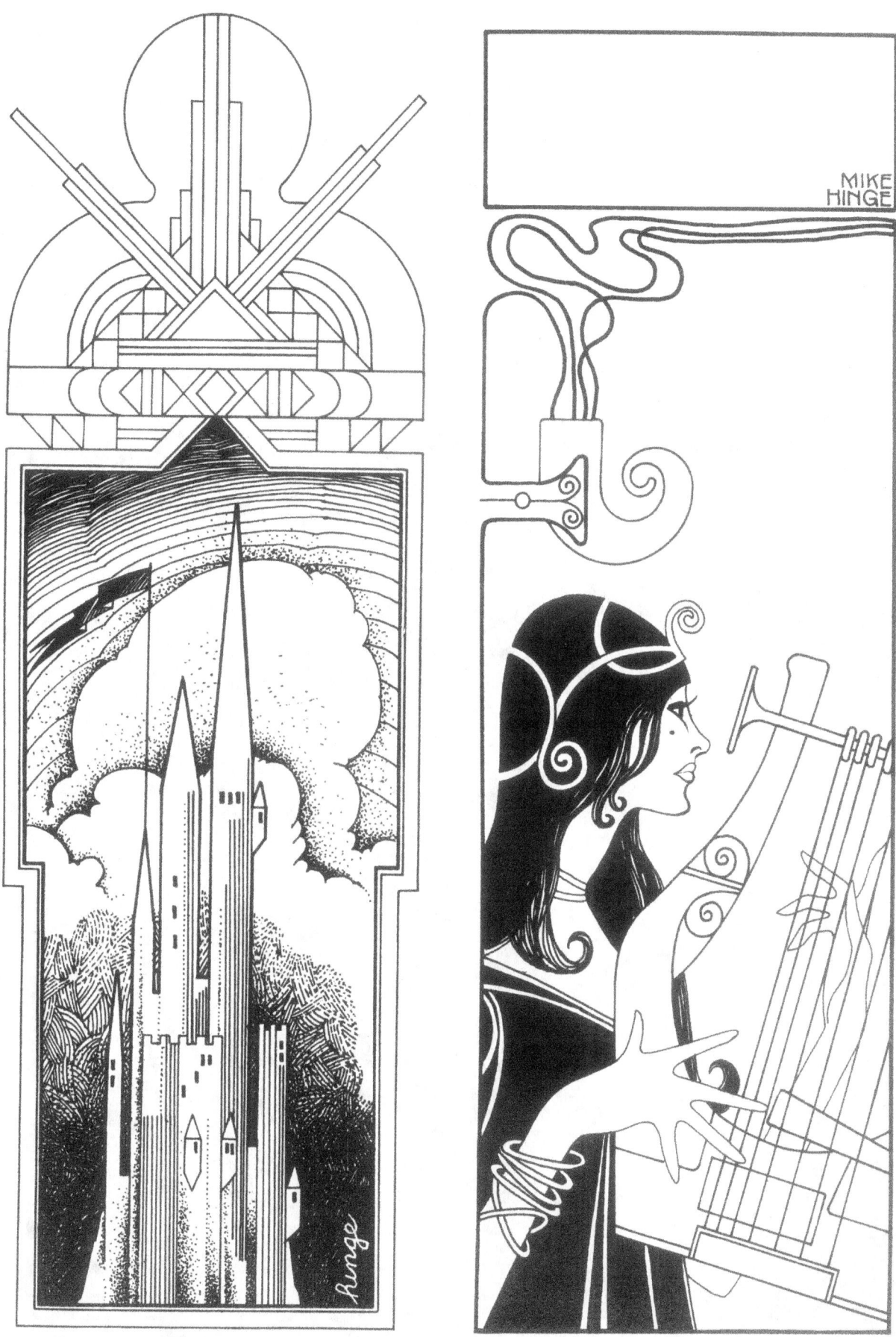

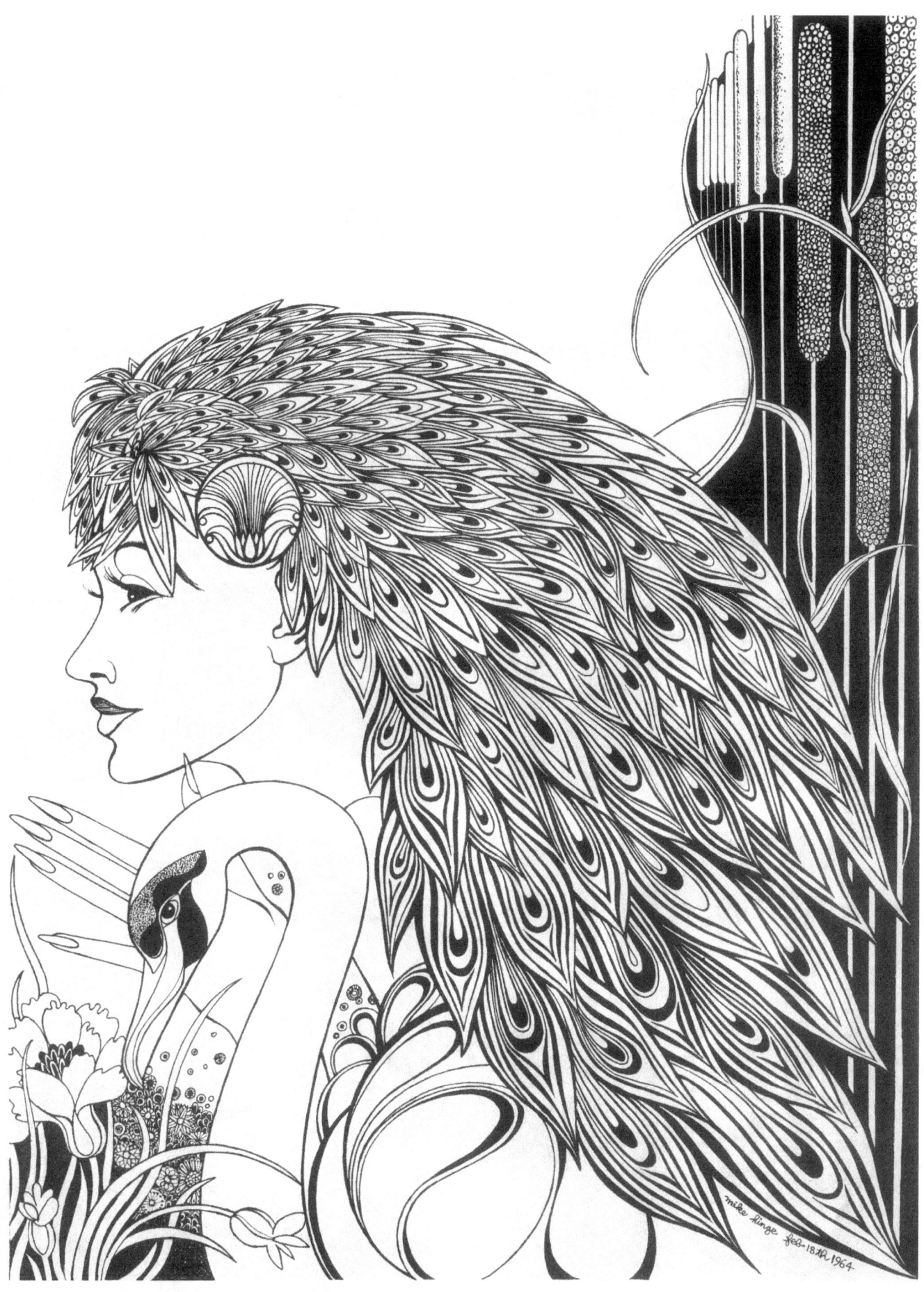

mike linge feb-18th 1964

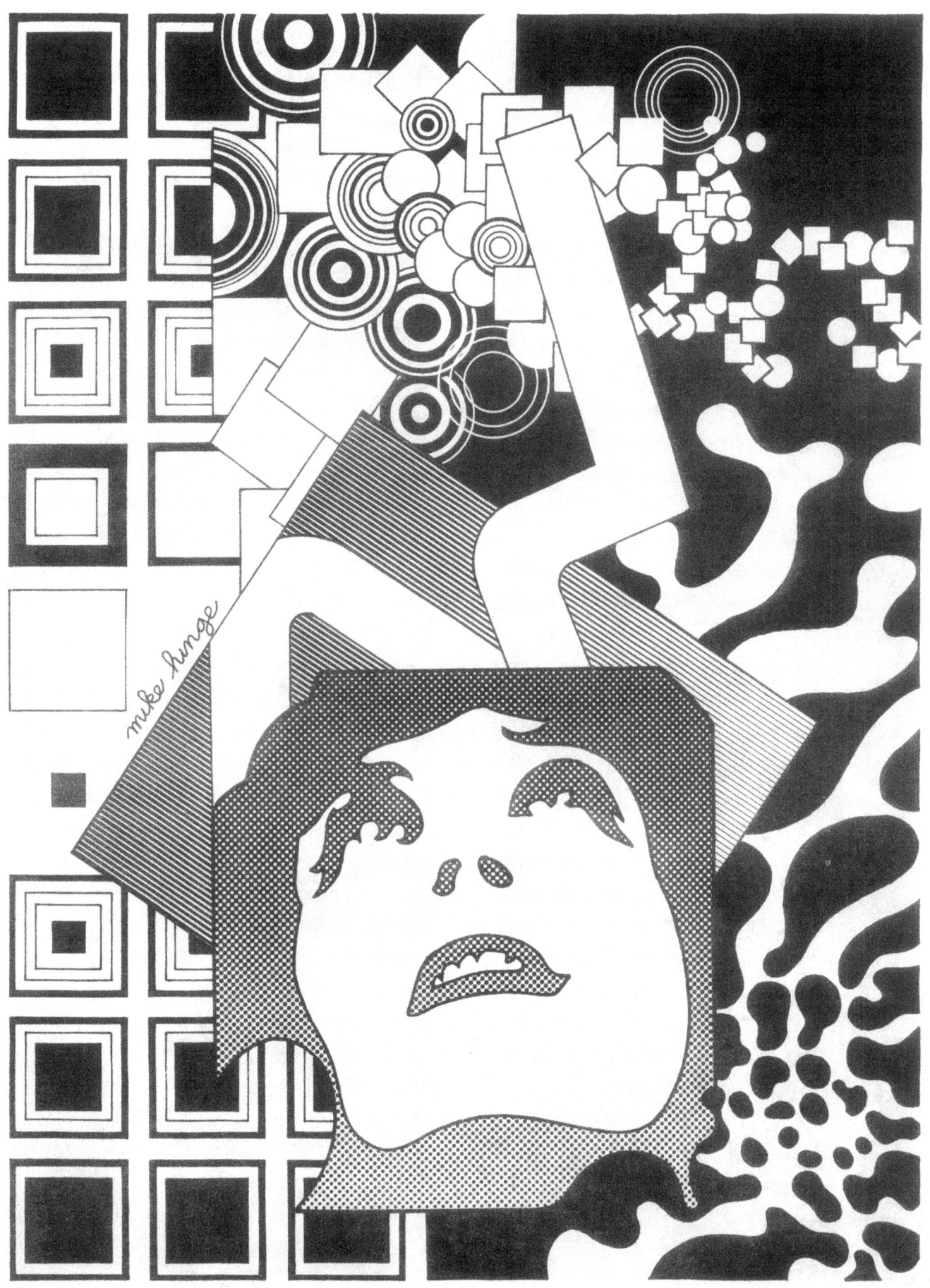

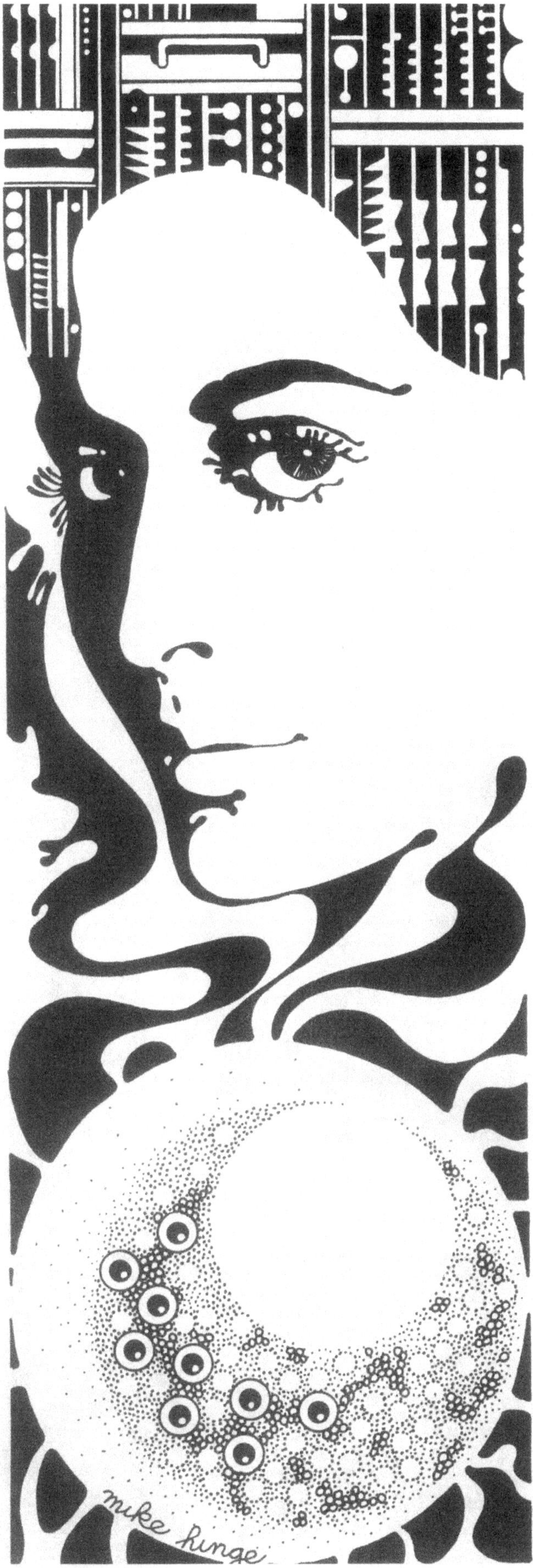

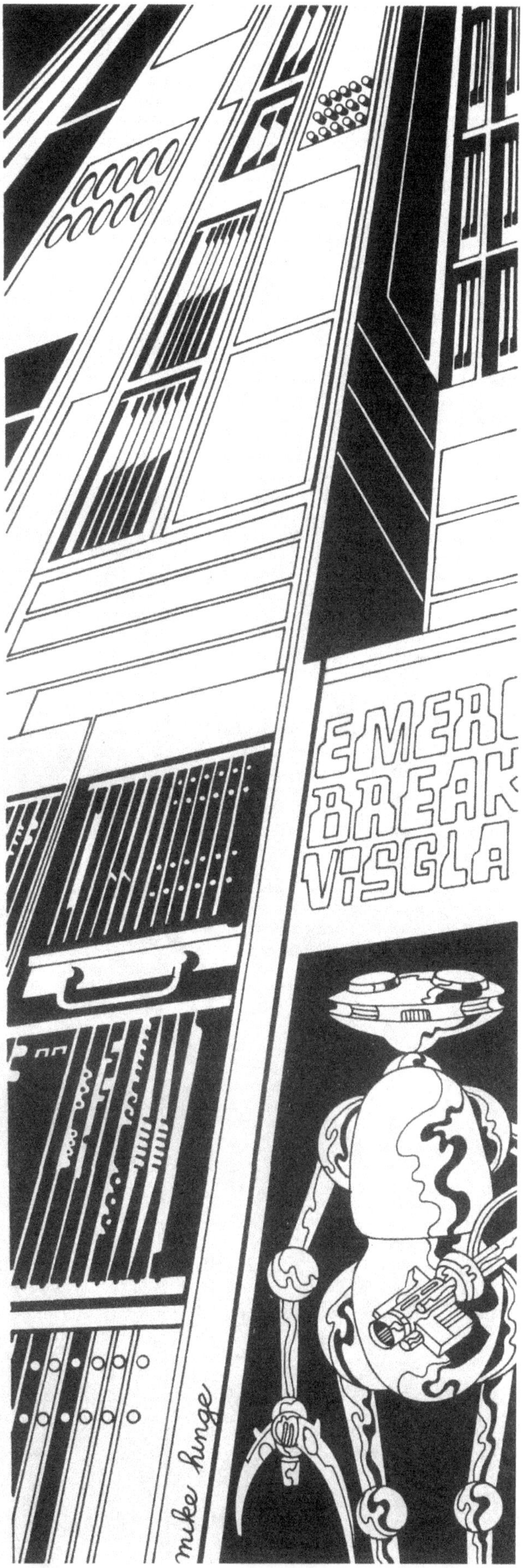

EMER
BREAK
VISGLA

mike hinge

mike hinge

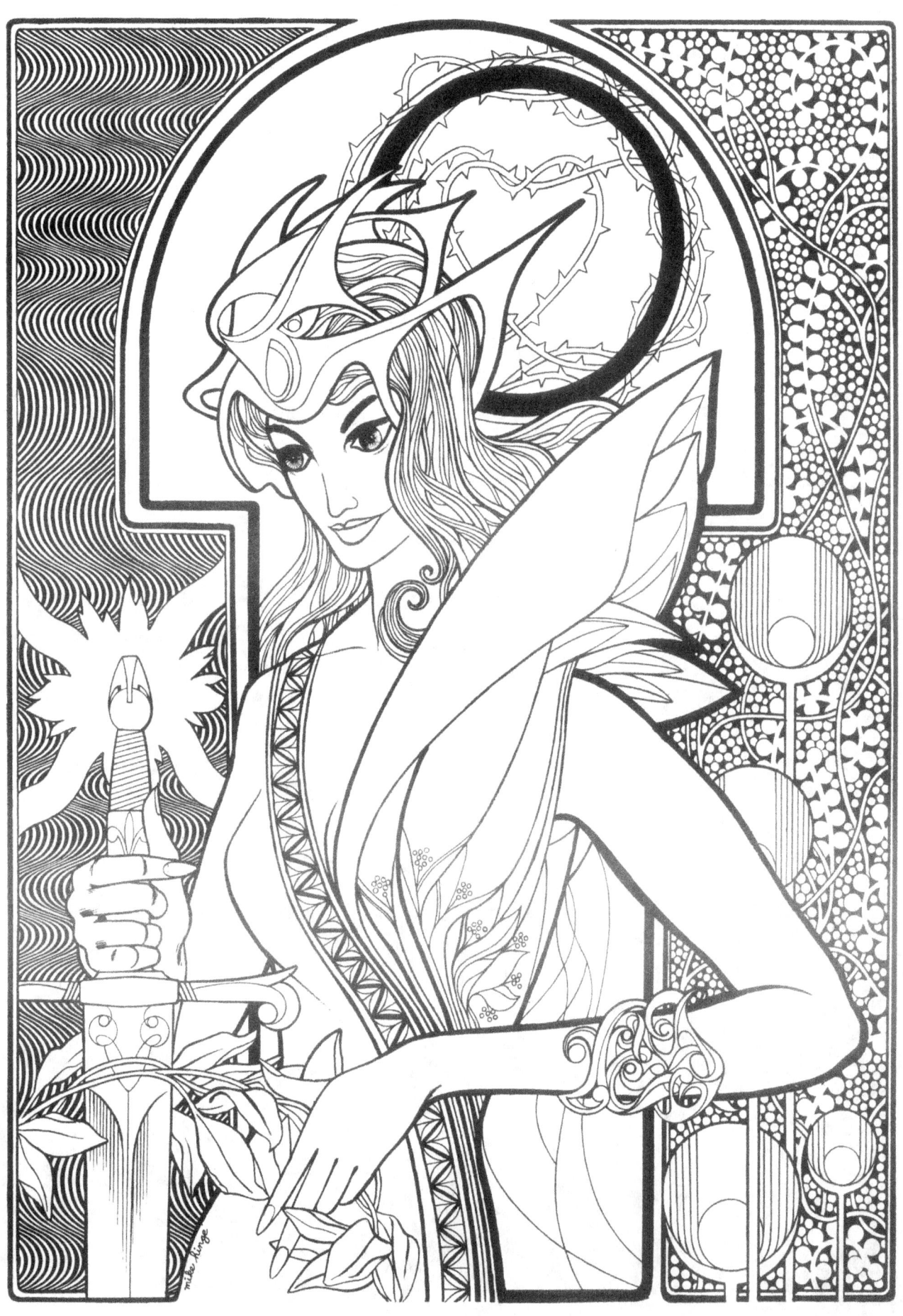

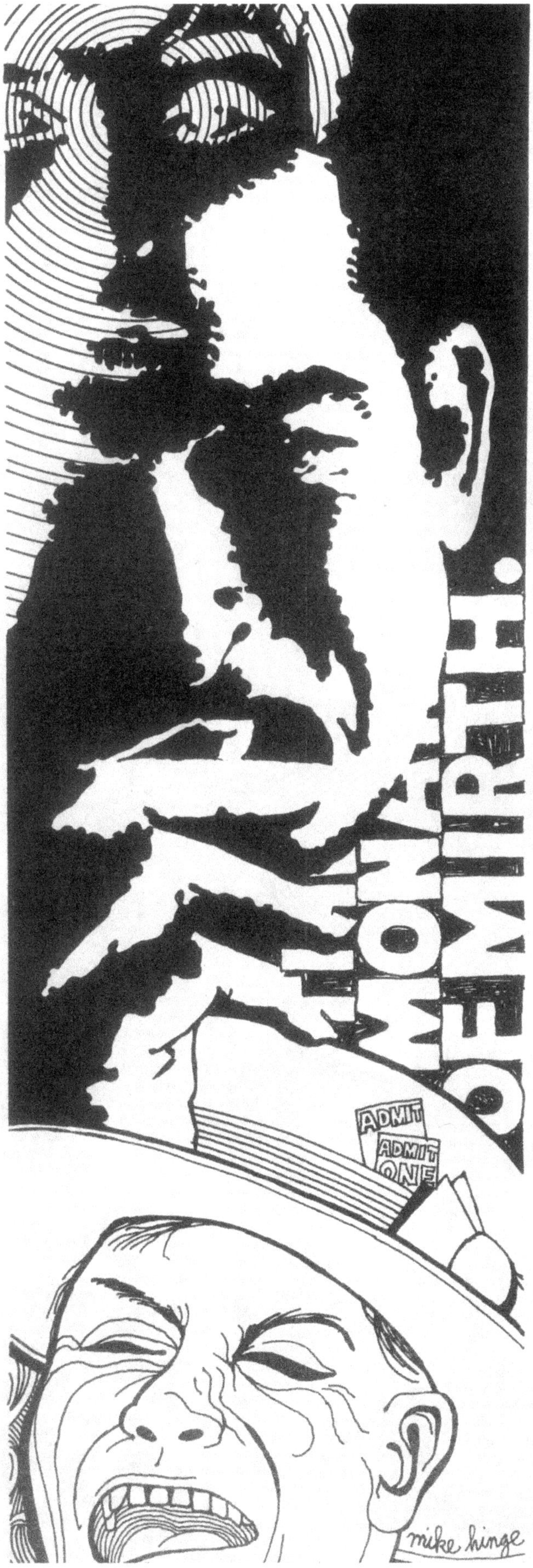
MONK
OF MIRTH.
ADMIT
ADMIT ONE
mike hinge

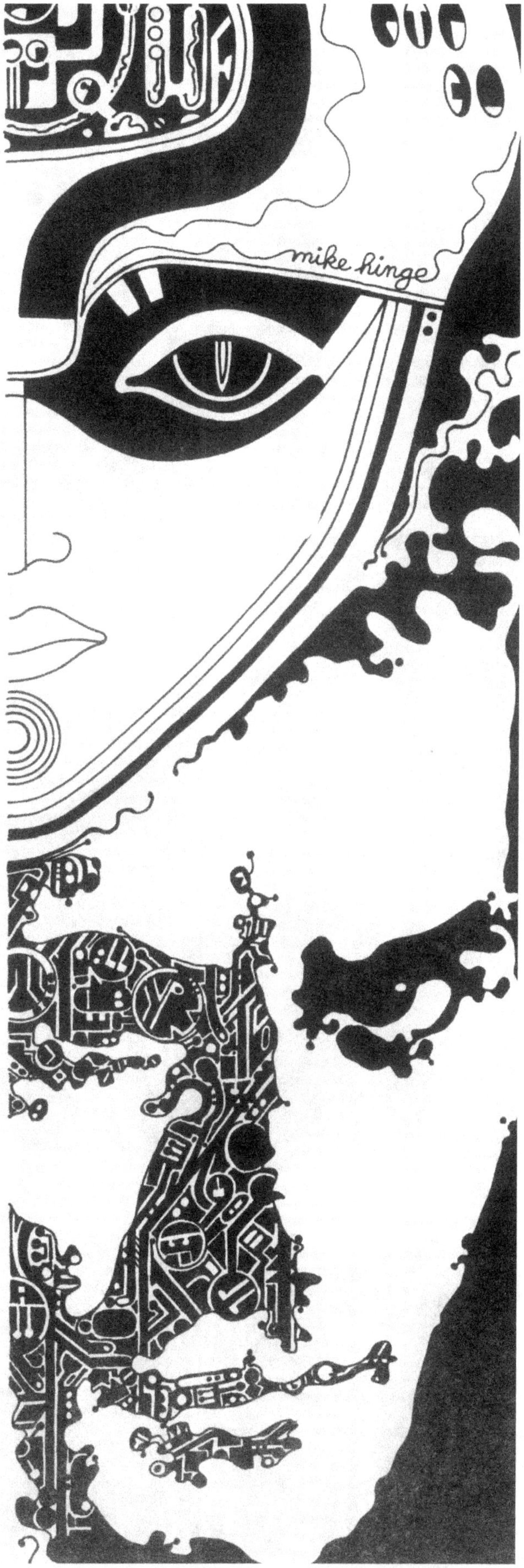
mike hinge

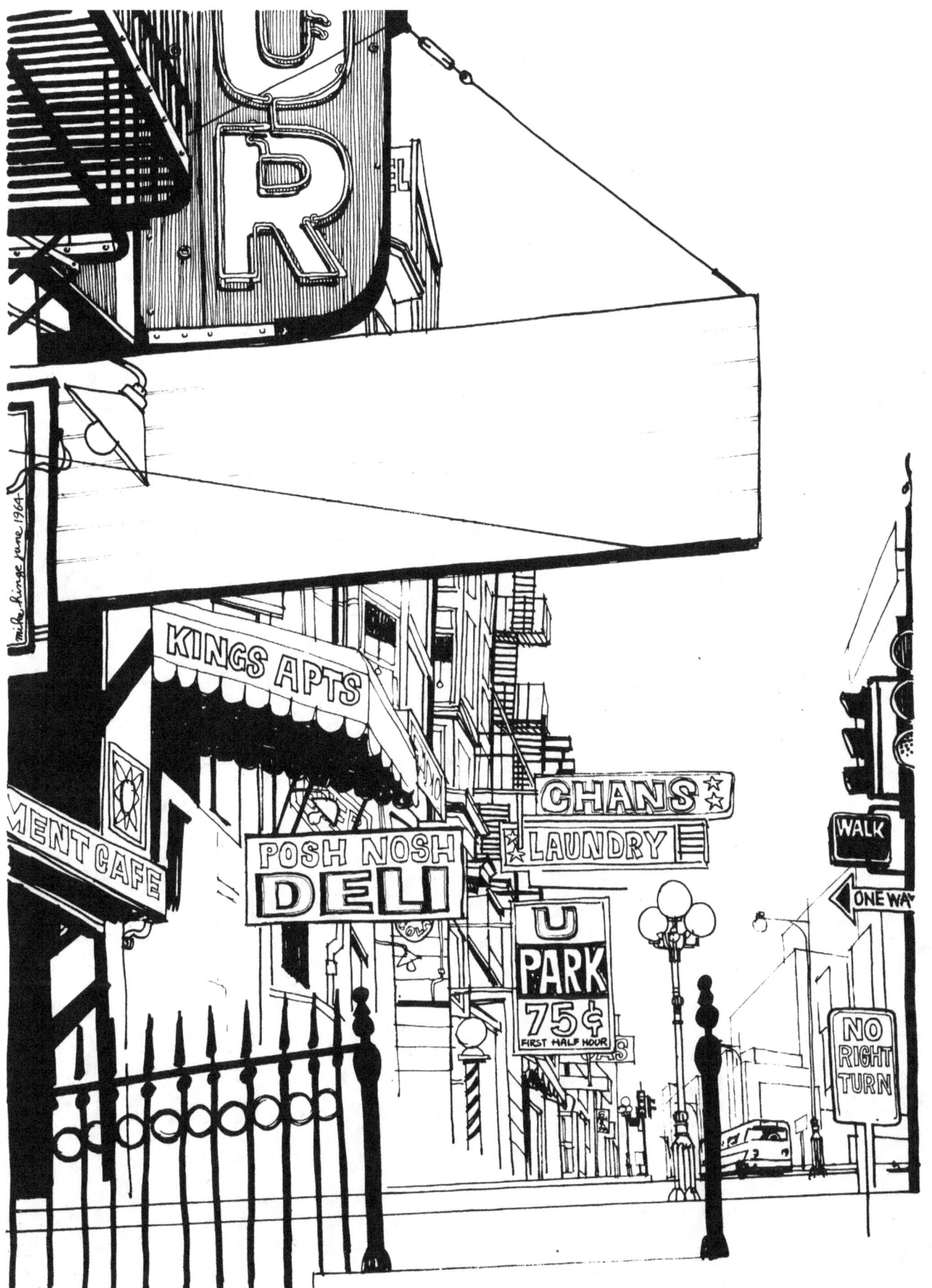

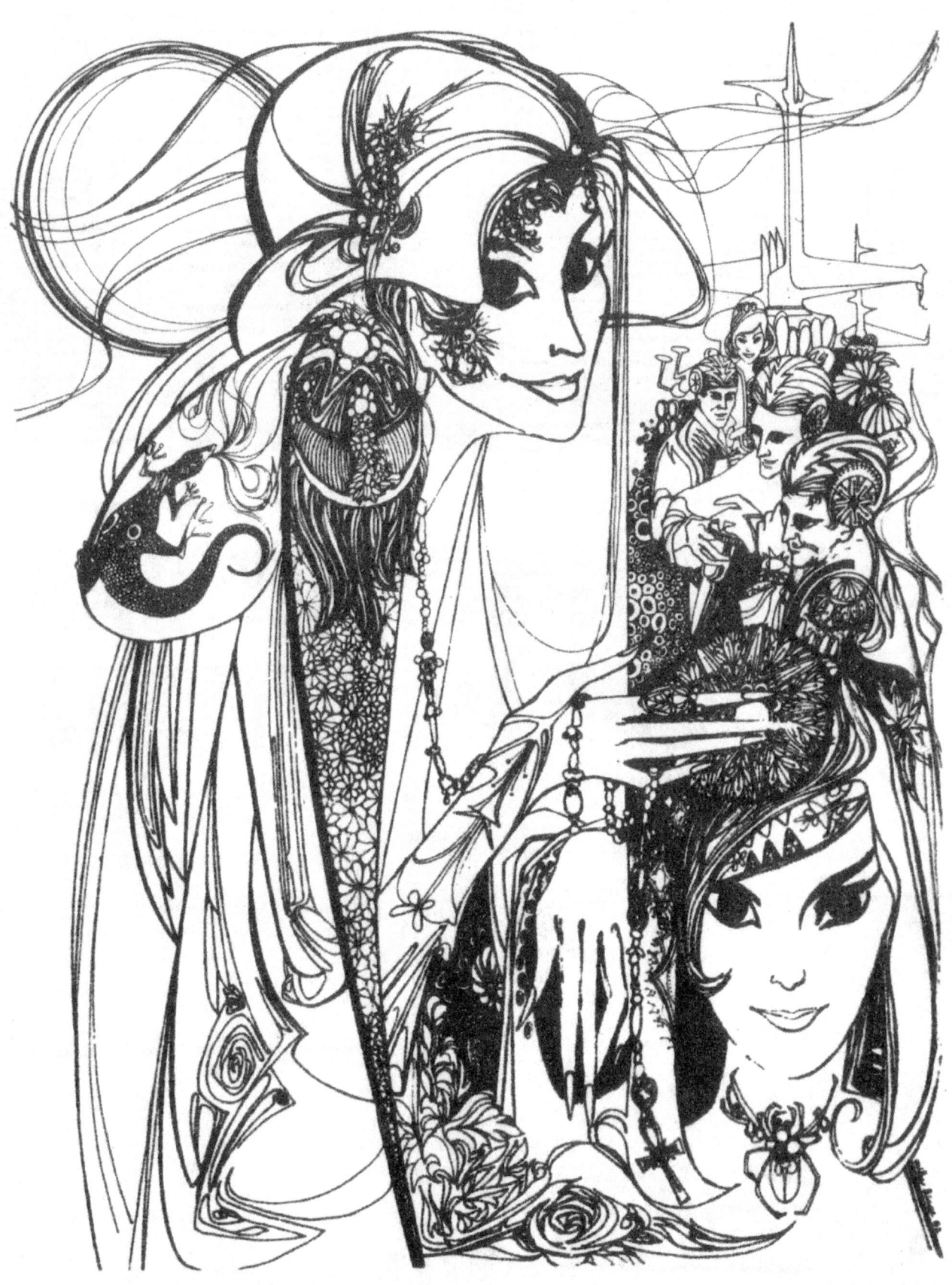

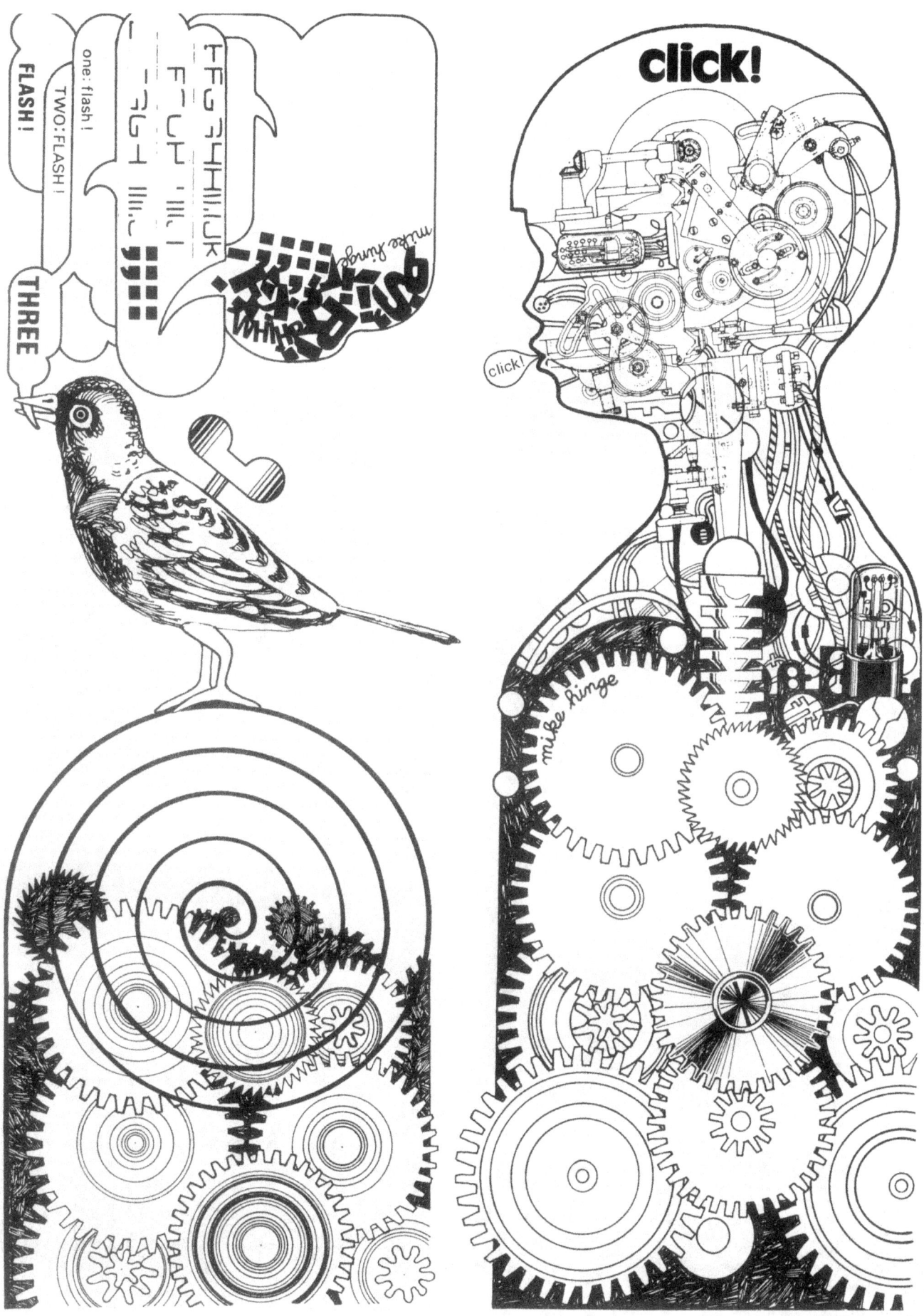

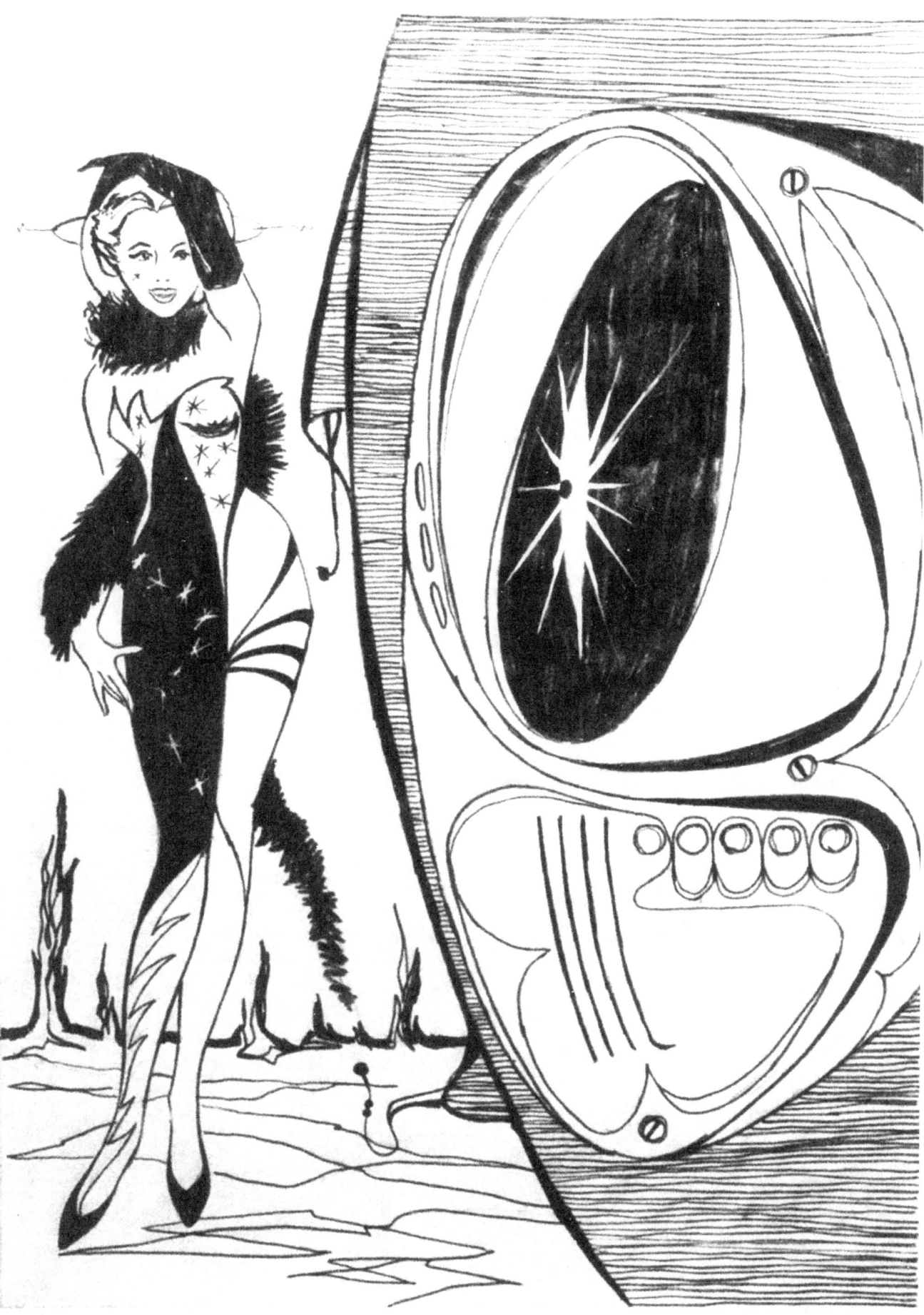

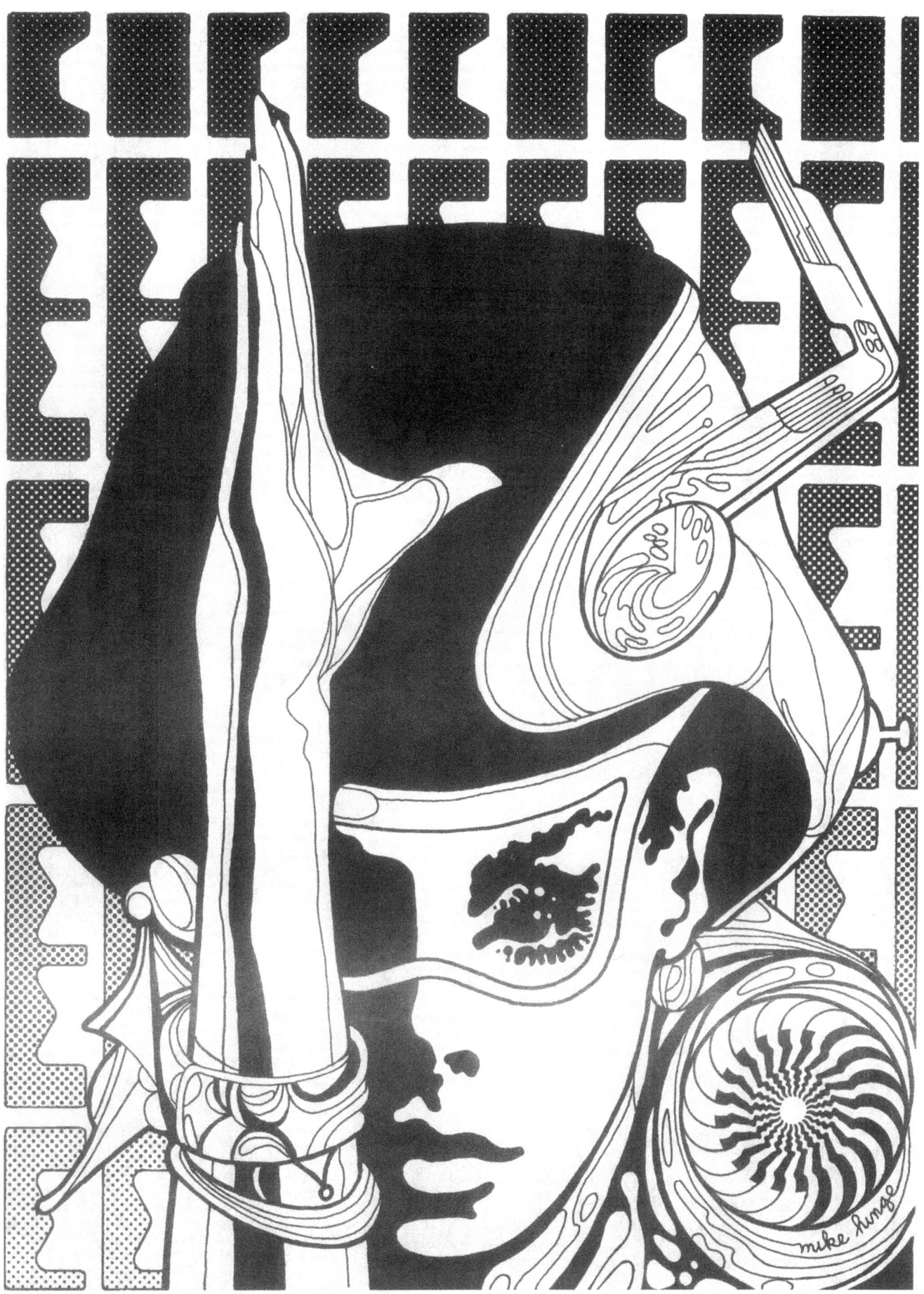

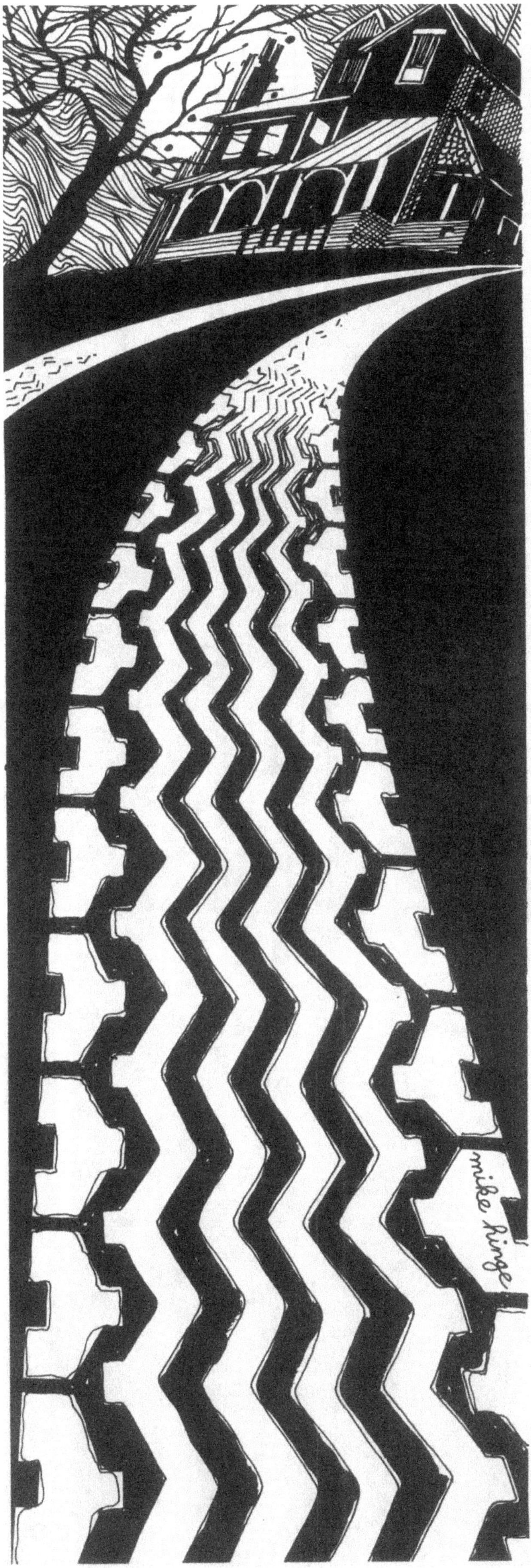

mike hinge

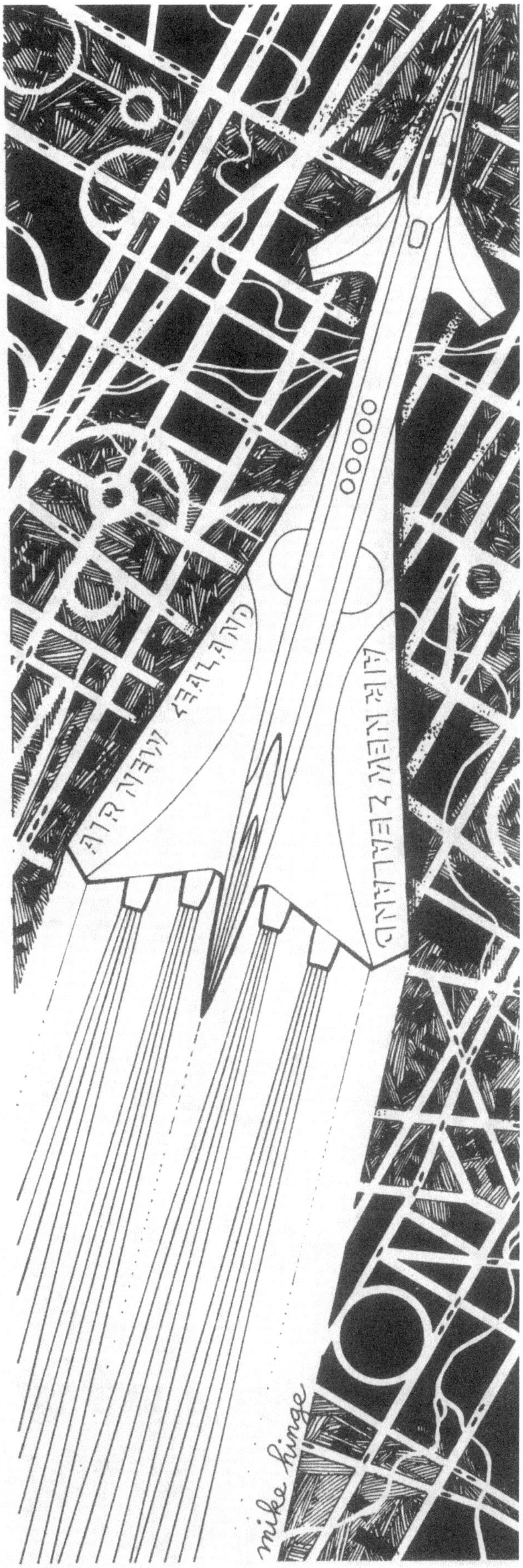

AIR NEW ZEALAND

AIR NEW ZEALAND

mike hinge

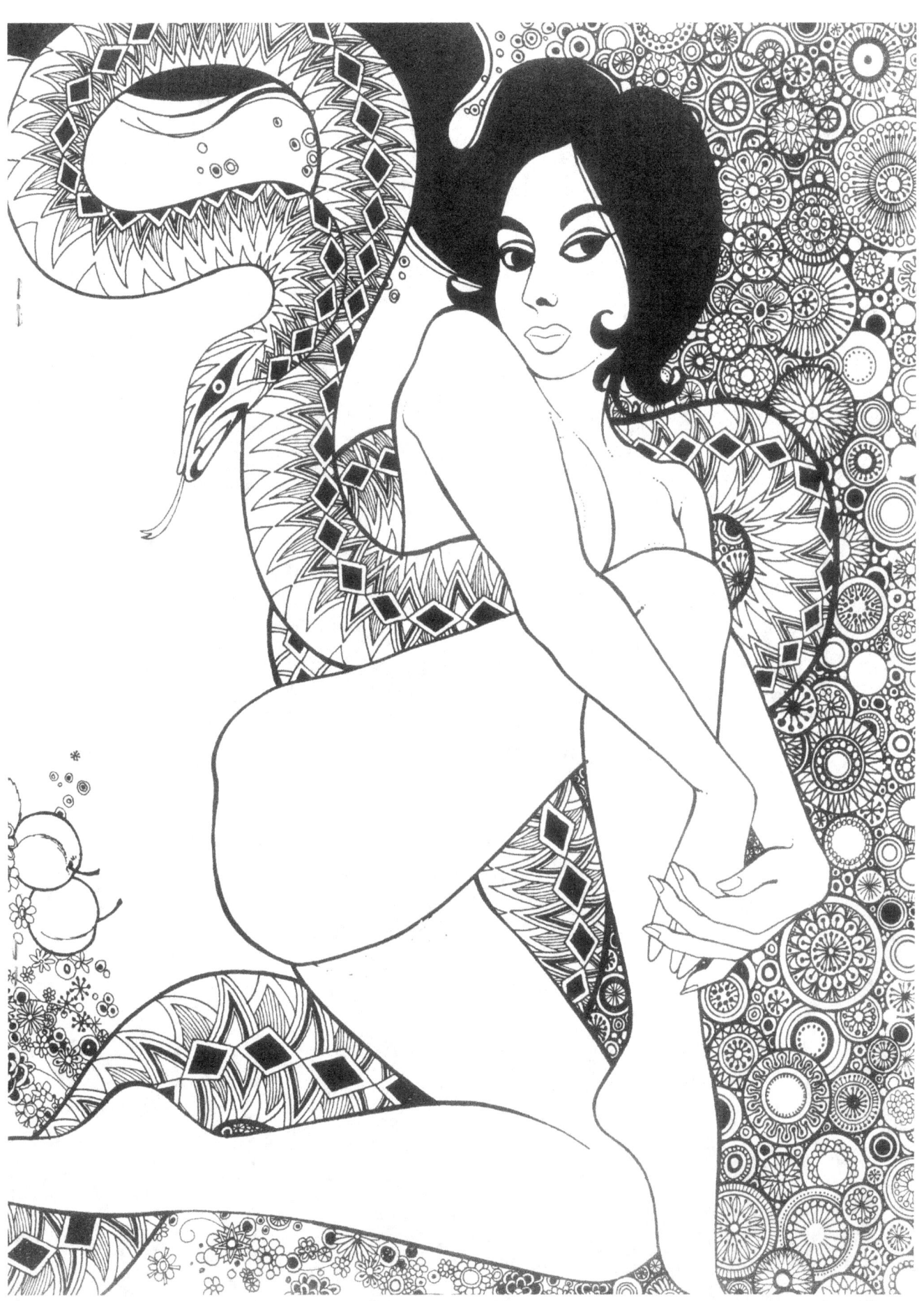

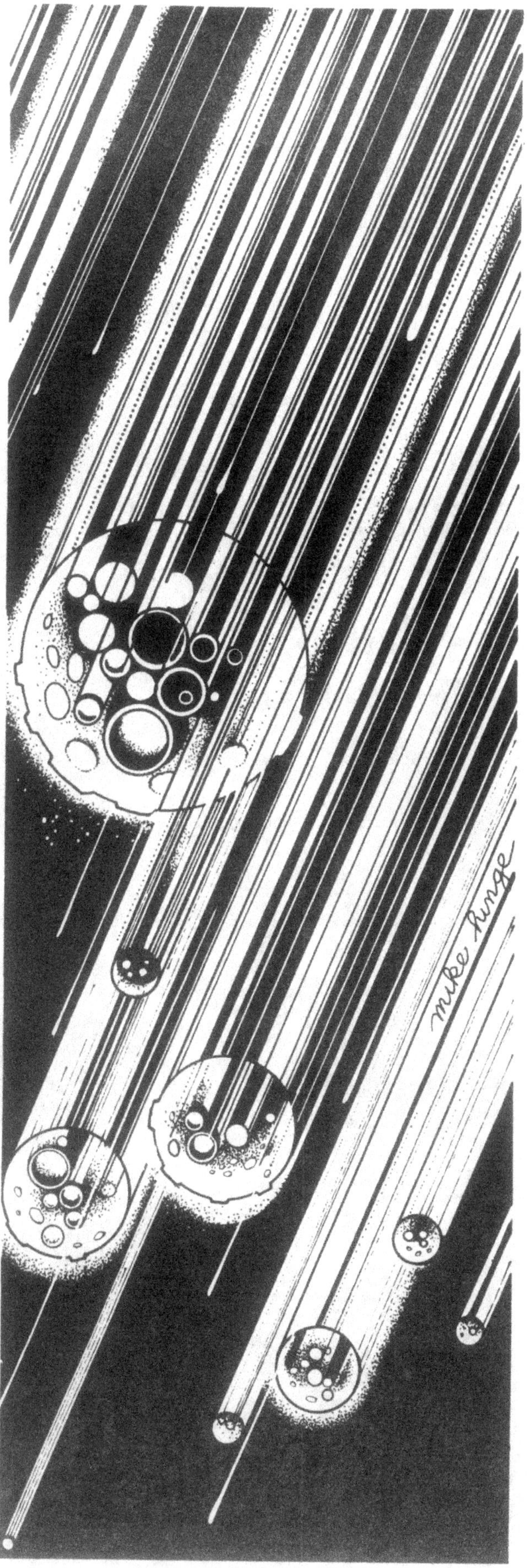
mike hinge

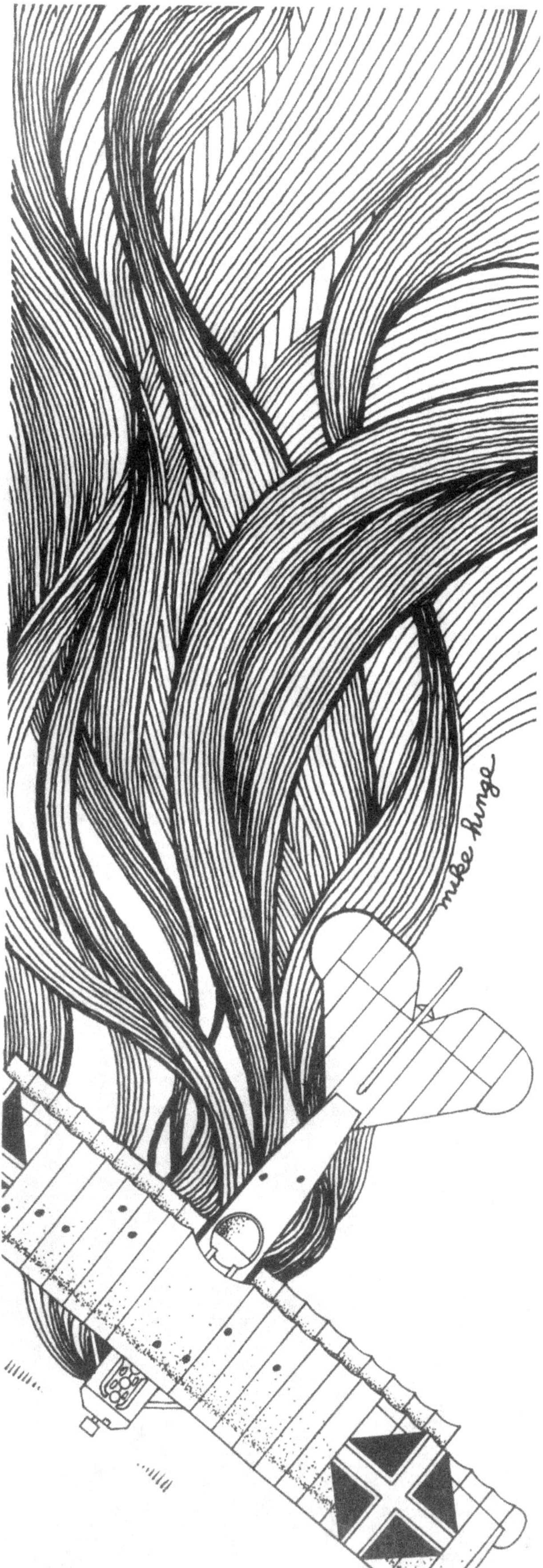
mike hinge

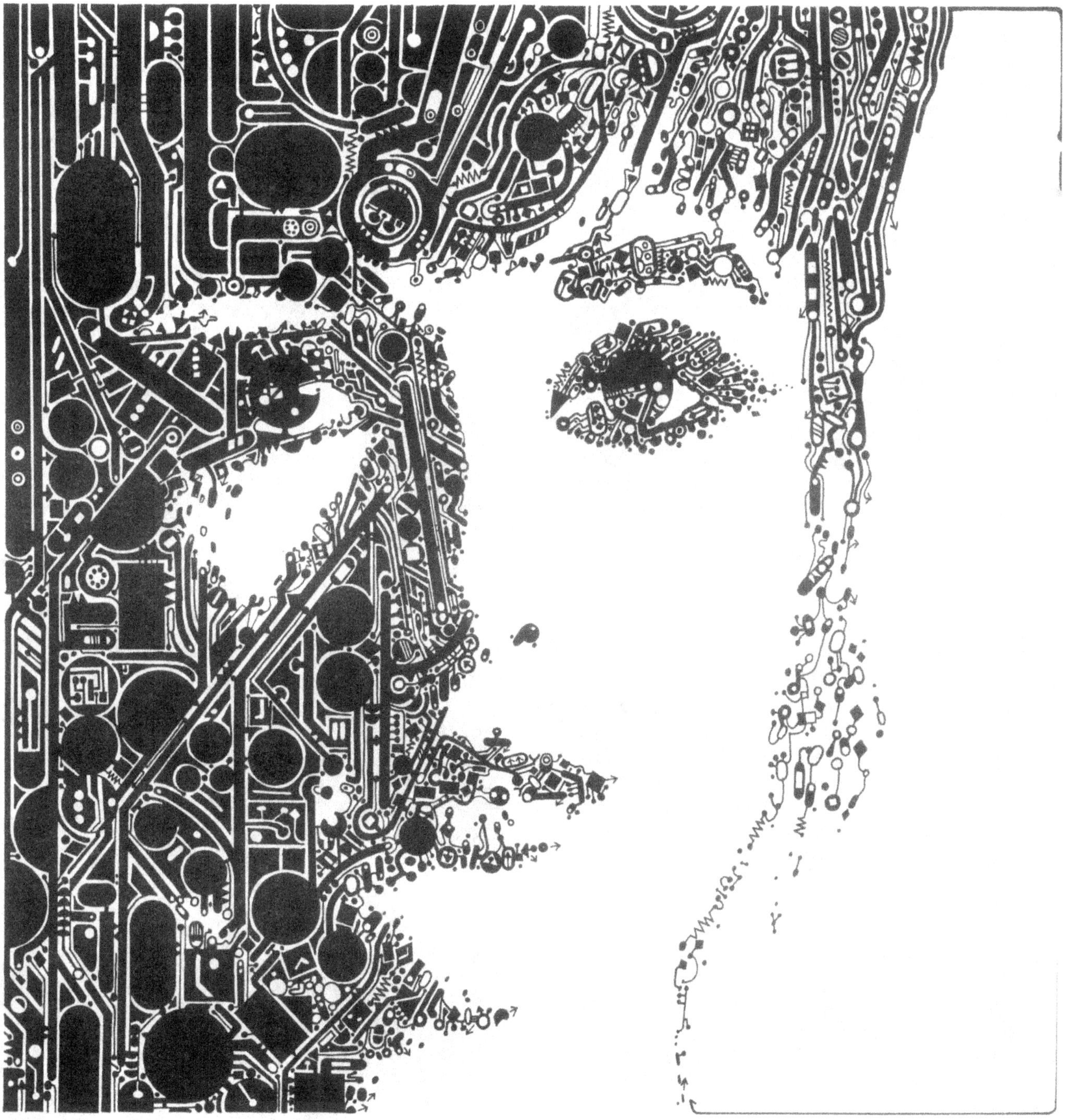

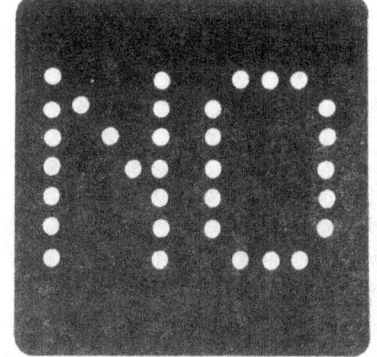 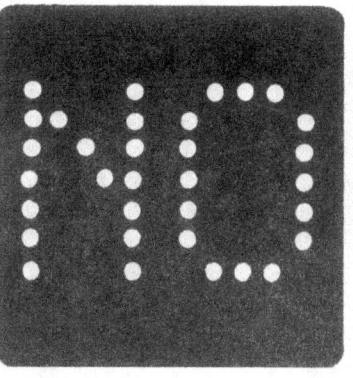 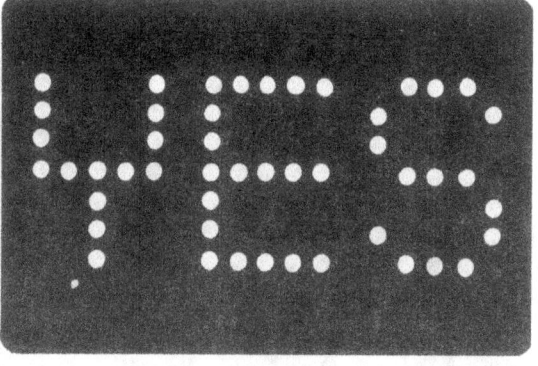

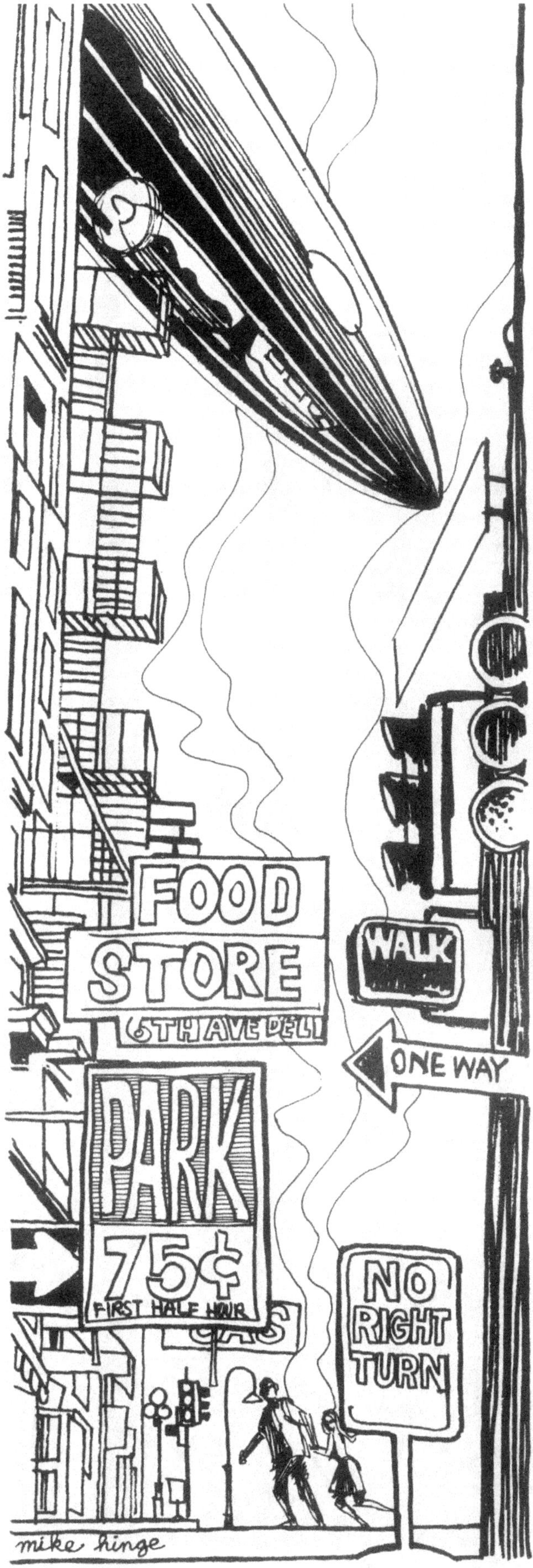

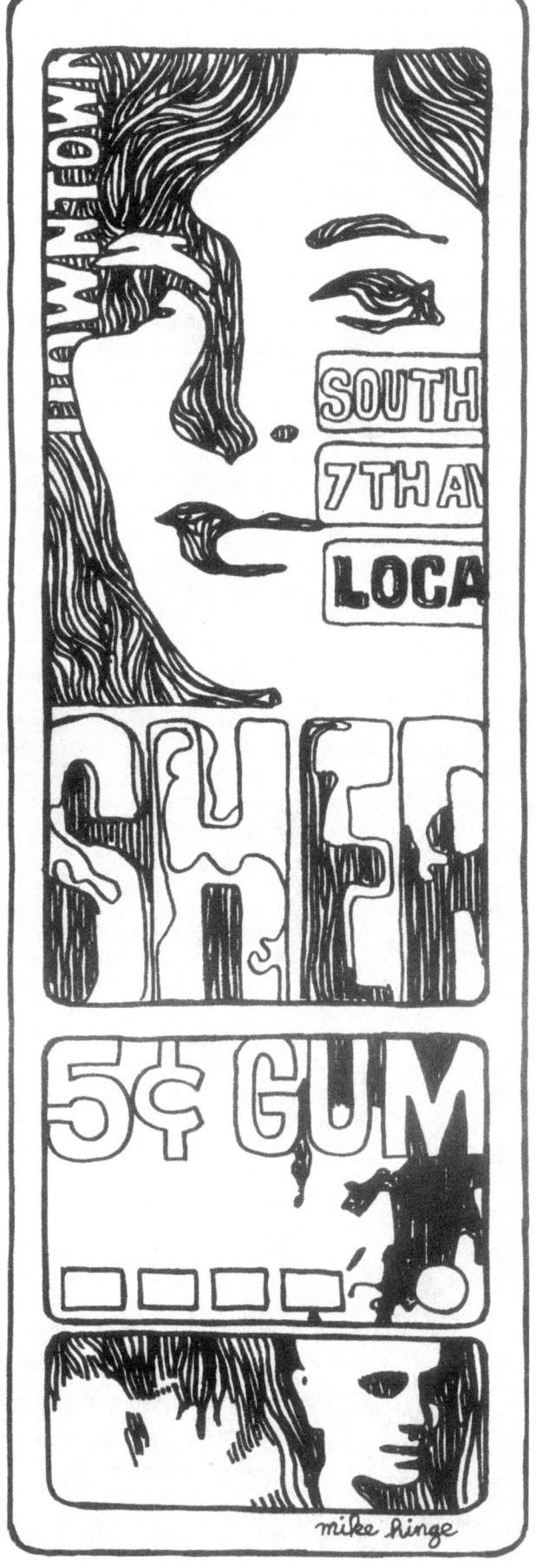

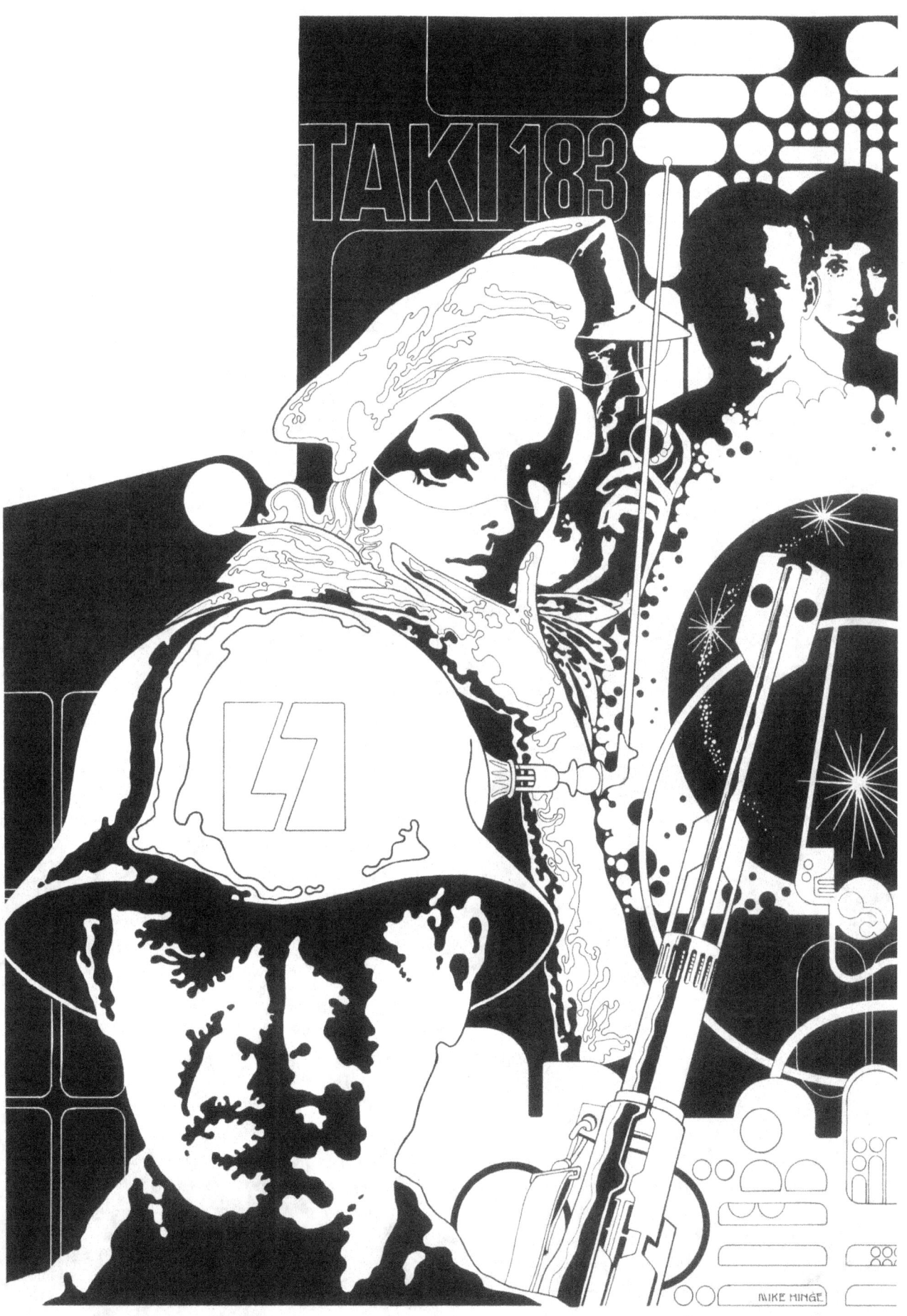

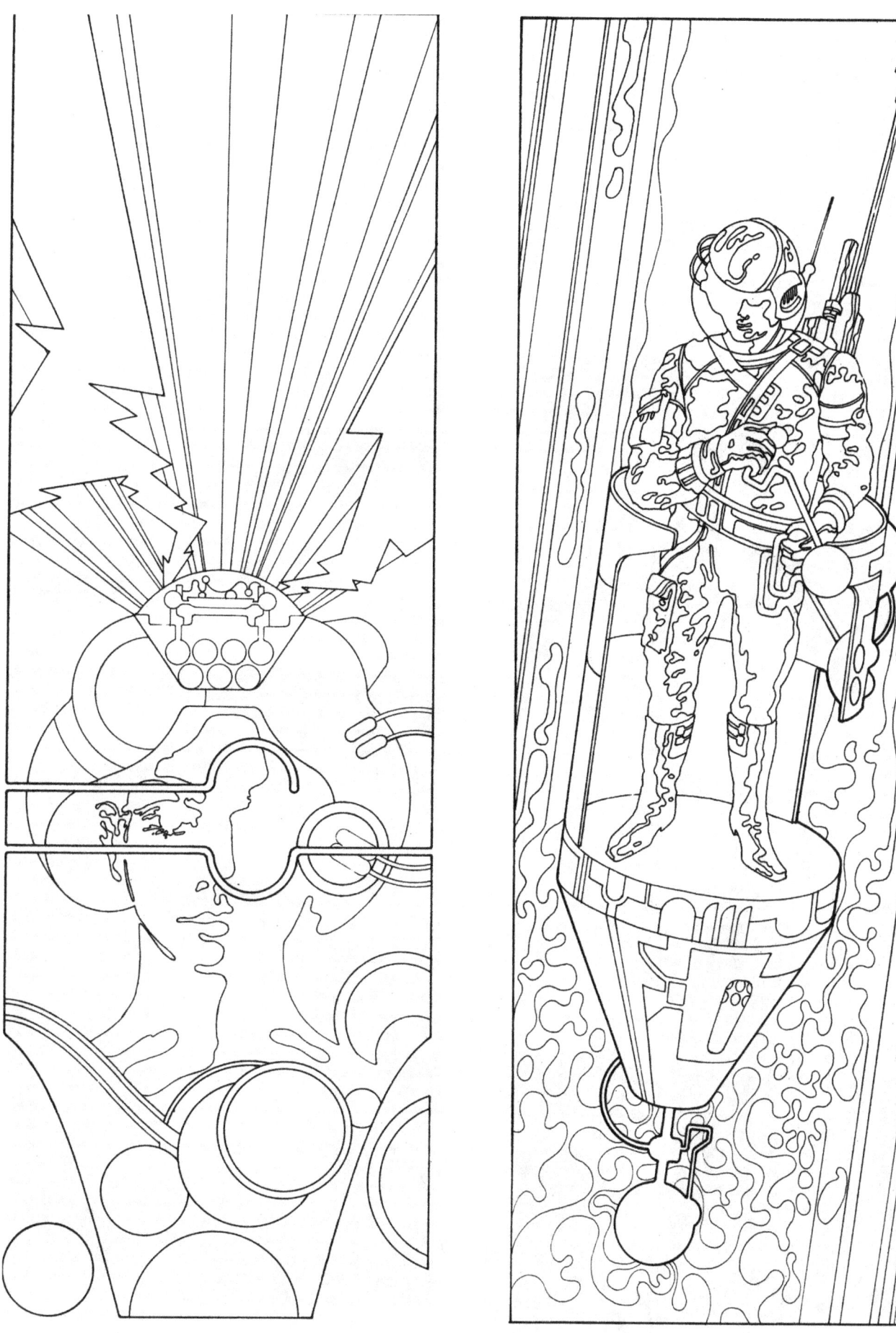

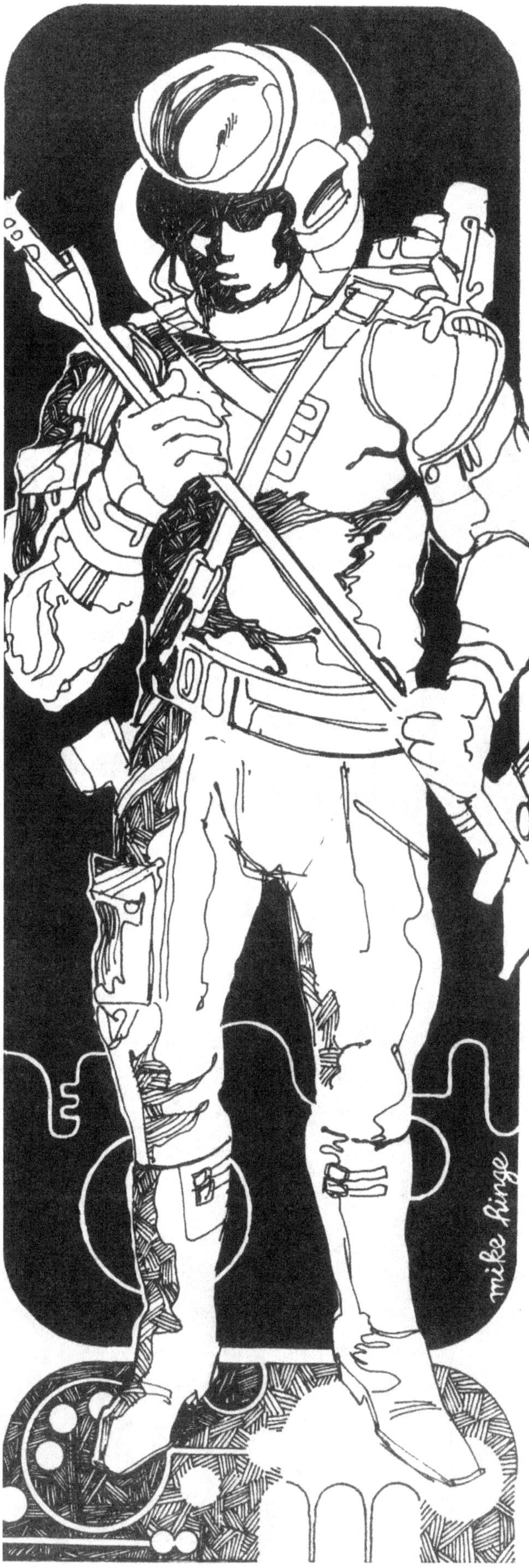

mike Ringe

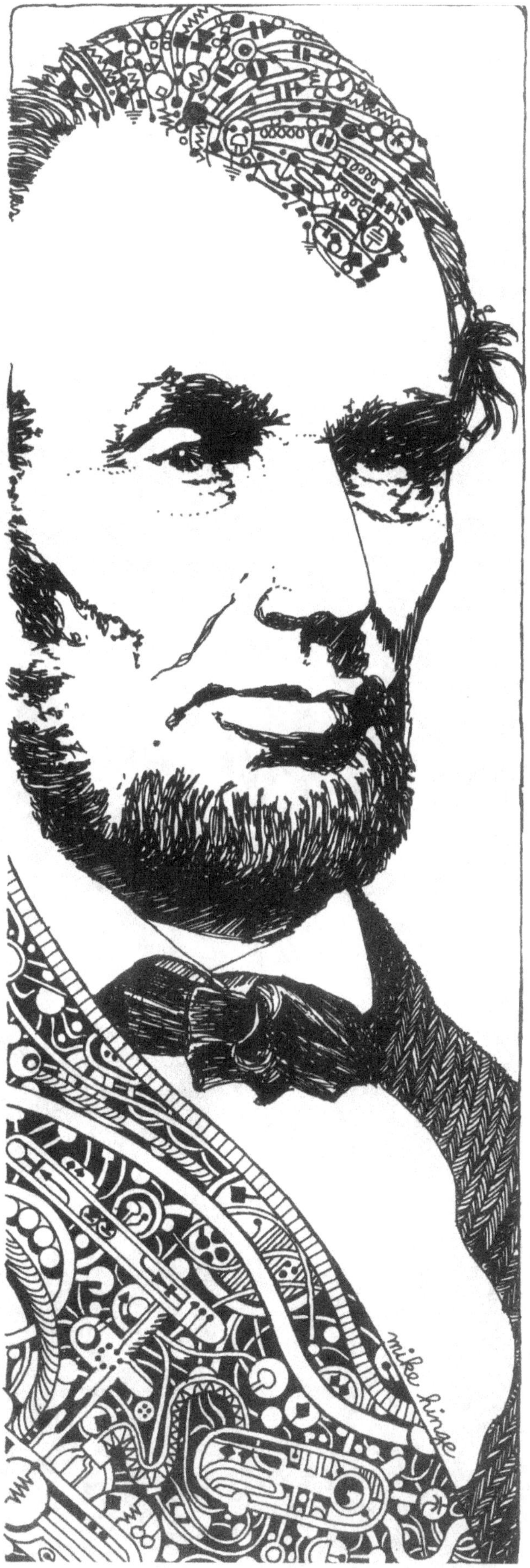

mike Ringe

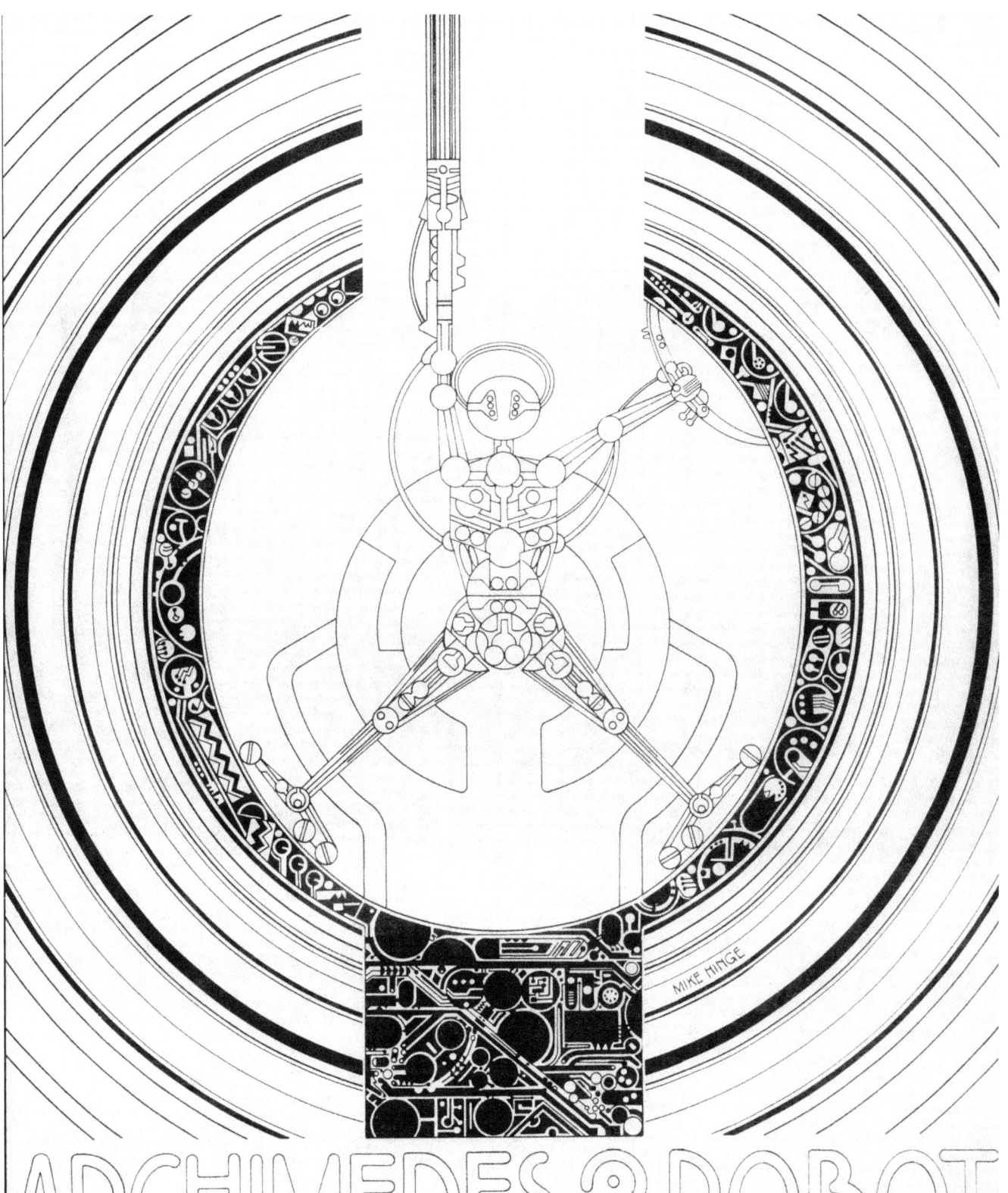

ARCHIMEDES 2 ROBOT

MIKE HINGE

A SEMICONDUCTOR FOR YOUR ELECTRONYX SYMPHONY
QUAVERED & SWORE ARRANGEMENTS IN 256 FOUR-BIT
WORDS, A CORP OF MM 521'S RAISED IN A THRENODY
WHISPERED DATA IN SILICONE DIOXIDE FUMING IN UNISON

A TRIBE OF 400-MHZ GERMANIAN AMPLIFIERS SCREAM
A FREQUENCY OPERA IN LYDIAN IMPEDANCE. THE BASS
SPUTTER OF CAPACITORS IN CONVIVAL HARMONY AS
TINTIBULATIONS OF TANTRIC HYBRIDS CHIP-IN ALTO